The Melungeons

The Resurrection of a Proud People

An Untold Story of Ethnic Cleansing in America

Second, revised, and corrected edition

by
N. Brent Kennedy

with
Robyn Vaughan Kennedy

Mercer University Press · Macon, Georgia USA

ISBN 0-86554-516-2　　　　　　　　　　　　　　　MUP/P143

The Melungeons.
The Resurrection of a Proud People.
An Untold Story of Ethnic Cleansing in America.
Second, revised, and corrected edition
Copyright ©1997
Mercer University Press, Macon, Georgia USA
Printed in the United States of America

The paper used in this publication meets the minimum
requirements of American National Standard
for Information Sciences—Permanence of Paper
for Printed Library Materials, ANSI Z39.48–1984.

Library of Congress Cataloging-in-Publication Data

CIP

The Melungeons

The Resurrection
of a Proud People

Typical Melungeon features are apparent in these representatives, past and present. <u>Center</u>, "Uncle Will" Collins, the author's great-great-uncle; <u>top left</u>, Wickliff Nash, ca. 1864; <u>top right</u>, Conley "Trig" Nash, son of Wickliff Nash and Louisa Hall Nash; <u>bottom left</u>, Nera and Kenneth Kennedy, children of N. B. Kennedy and Tessie Colley Kennedy; and <u>bottom right</u>, the author, N. Brent Kennedy.

Contents

Dedication

to all people of Melungeon descent

who are living evidence of the human will to survive,
standing tall among their neighbors
as teachers, farmers, doctors, and miners,
all bearing witness to the indomitable spirit
of their early American forebears.

Preface

The Melungeons: The Resurrection of a Proud People is the first volume in a planned series of informational works on the Melungeons and other related peoples of Appalachia. Although it is a highly personalized work and not intended as an academic treatise, to some degree it is an outgrowth of my involvement with the Melungeon Research Committee. Created in mid-1992, this team of investigators examining the Melungeon mystery is comprised of internationally respected scholars and talented laypeople, a number of whom are Melungeon.

Inasmuch as additional research is presently being conducted on the history, origins, and lore of the Melungeons, many of the theories discussed in this book are consequently subject to change. The reader should bear this in mind. Also, the opinions expressed in this book represent my personal thinking and should not be considered as necessarily representative of the Melungeon Research Committee.

Given the unavoidably cautious and time-consuming nature of academic research, I am confident that many exciting discoveries await us. I do not want this book to be interpreted as the final word on the Melungeons. It is not. I do believe, however, that the hypotheses presented here closely parallel the present thinking of many of the members of the committee. So, in this respect, I am comfortable discussing them in a public forum.

Given the deluge of requests for more information on the Melungeons, and having evolved into a sort of personal clearing house for much of the study results being reported, I decided to publish *The Melungeons: The Resurrection of a Proud People* as both a preliminary report on our knowledge base to date, and as a way to bring a little sanity to my homelife. During any given week, I receive between thirty and fifty requests for information on the Melungeons, to all of which I have diligently tried to respond. This has not been easy. This book seemed the best way to simultaneously assist people in their own search, as well as bring a sense of order to my own increasingly hectic schedule.

I strongly emphasize that I am not a historian, an anthropologist, or a professional writer. I continue to need—and energetically seek—the assistance of others. If there are errors in my work, or if any readers have information or insight that could further refine or illuminate the sometimes hesitant conclusions in these pages, please share that information with me and I will see that it is incorporated into our research.

There is no pride of authorship here, nor an agenda to prove any particular point of view or heritage for that matter. What I most want is simply to establish as much of the truth as possible, and then let each individual make up his or her own mind. And while I feel strongly that my conclusions will indeed be born out by future scholars, I have been and remain open to any and all possibilities.

In writing about the Melungeons, I have of necessity drawn from the history of my own family, which I have discovered is not unlike the histories of other Melungeon families. I hope it will prove both enlightening and emotionally comforting to those with a personal interest in the topic. And, of even greater importance, perhaps the sharing of my family's "darkest secrets" will spur others to engage in their own family sleuthing, and thus add even more to our understanding of the history and culture of the Melungeon people.

Acknowledgments

As with any written work, there are always others than the one whose name appears on the title page who merit special mention for the support they have provided. In the case of *The Melungeons: The Resurrection of a Proud People*, there are many, far too many to include all their names here. However, a few merit special recognition and I would be remiss if I did not mention them. First and foremost, my wife and son, whose editorial and moral support were unparalleled. Thank you, Robyn and Ryan. To my mother, father, and my brother Richard (who suspected the truth long before I did), and to my aunts, uncles, and cousins I also say thank you, especially for your willingness to share private, sometimes painful memories with me. I promise it will serve a positive purpose beyond the simple retelling. And to all members of the Melungeon Research Team who have given so freely of their time, money, and energies to advance our understanding of the Melungeon people, thank you.

In particular, I especially appreciate the long hours and creativity applied to our work by Eloy and Anne Gallegos (and look forward to Eloy's upcoming book on the Spanish influence on the Southeast); Dr. Jefferson Chapman of the University of Tennessee; Dr. Chester DePratter of the University of South Carolina, principal humanities scholar for the Melungeon Research Committee; Evelyn McKinley Orr of Omaha, Nebraska; Scott Collins of Sneedville, Tennessee; Debbie Wolfe of Oregon; Terry Brennan of Herndon, Virginia; Dr. Robert Gilmer of Abingdon, Virginia; Ruth Johnson of Kingsport, Tennessee; Arlee Gowen of Lubbock, Texas; Jack Goins of Rogersville, Tennessee; Dr. Sayyid M. Syeed, general-secretary of the Islamic Society of North America; Dr. Shahid Athar of Indianapolis, Indiana; the Honorable Nuzhet Kandemir, ambassador of Turkey; Louis de Sousa of the embassy of Portugal; Portuguese researchers Manuel Mira and Fernanda Lopes; and relatives Vernoy Moore, Helen Nash Mayo, R. E. Stallard, and Evelyn Stallard Smith of Coeburn Mountain, Virginia. I also extend my grateful appreciation to Bill VanDerKloot of VanDerKloot Film & Television in Atlanta for his tireless support of my various Melungeon-related projects. And to my good friends Peter Karp and Mehmet Topcak, for their patience, dependable objectivity, and consistently sound advice.

To the South Carolina Humanities Council, the Georgia Humanities Council, the Kentucky Humanities Council, and the Virginia Foundation for the Humanities and Public Policy, all of which provided early, crucial grant support for the work of the committee. And especially to Elaine Freeman of South Carolina Educational Television and Dr. Randy Akers of the South Carolina Humanities Council. Their early, personal encouragement when others scoffed literally gave me the strength to continue plodding ahead.

I must also say a special thank you to Jean Patterson Bible and the late Bonnie Ball, whose groundbreaking work in accurately and sensitively preserving our Melungeon heritage has not only been invaluable, but has served as a benchmark for those of us who are trying to continue where they left off. Their books remain must reading for any serious student of Melungeon culture and history.

And to those journalists who have been particularly diligent and conscientious in reporting the work of our committee: Mario Crespo, Washington, D.C. bureau chief of Radio-Television Portugal; Chris Wohlwend of the *Atlanta Journal-Constitution*; Bruce Henderson of the *Charlotte Observer*; the late Barbara Watson of the *Kingsport* (Tennessee) *Times-News*; Brad Lifford of the

Kingsport Times-News; Dana Beyerle of the Montgomery bureau of the *New York Times*; Kenneth Adkins and Tabatha Mullins of the *Bristol* (Virginia) *Herald-Courier*; Knoxville, Tennessee broadcast journalist Bill Landry of the Heartland Series; Jennifer Rose, Jeff Lester, and Mike Still of the *Coalfield Progress* in Norton, Virginia; Greg Wallace of WCYB-TV in Bristol, Virginia; Raul Rivera of WUSA-Gannett-T.V. in Washington, D.C.; David Osier of the *Georgia Journal*; Omer Bin Abdulla of *Islamic Horizons*; Savas Süzal of SABAH and A-TV (Turkey); Baris Manco of *From 7 to 77* (Turkey); Byron Crawford of the *Louisville Courier-Journal*; Ethma Odum of KALB-TV, Alexandria, Louisana; and Maurice Talbot and Mary Lou Harcharic of the University of North Carolina Center for Public Television, in Research Triangle Park.

And finally, to the more than two thousand individuals who during the past six years have shared their theories, genealogies, and family histories. Each of you is an integral part of the Melungeon story and I look forward to our continued journey together.

O there are voices of the past,
links of a broken chain,
wings that can bear me back to times
which cannot come again;
Yet God forbid that I should lose
the echoes that remain!

—author unknown

Introduction

This is the story of my family, and by way of tangled kinship, many other families with roots on the Cumberland Plateau of Virginia, Kentucky, North Carolina, West Virginia, and Tennessee. But more important, in a very real way it is also the story of a people. A people ravaged, and nearly destroyed, by the senseless excesses of racial prejudice and ethnic cleansing. A people of apparent Mediterranean descent who may have settled the Appalachian wilderness as early as 1567—forty years before Jamestown. A people who almost certainly intermarried with the Powhatans, Pamunkeys, Creeks, Catawbas, Yuchis, and Cherokees to form what some have called, perhaps a bit fancifully, "a new race." A people who built cabins and tilled the land, and, at least by the late 1700s, were practicing Christians. A people who were, a century and a half later, crushed and scattered beneath the violent onslaught of unbridled Anglo jingoism.

In historical fairness, these people suffered physical injustices that were no greater, and perhaps even less traumatic, than either Native Americans or African-Americans. However, unlike the majority of their Indian and African cousins, the Melungeons were dealt the additional insult of being robbed of their heritage. Ethnically and culturally raped, as it were.

In most instances, the Anglos did not assign a fictitious origin to the Cherokee or the African slave, being content that their

N. B. Kennedy,
author's grandfather, ca. 1930.

Tessie Colley Kennedy,
author's grandmother, 1929.

mere existence as a member of either group ensured disenfranchisement or enslavement. The Melungeons, however, were a different matter and a peculiar, more unsettling challenge. In order to pillage these dark-skinned, frustratingly European-looking people, who were often Christian to boot, a new heritage had to be invented. Never mind that from the earliest encounters the Melungeons seemed to know who they were—or that their claim of origin was a nonexotic, easily verifiable one. The truth after all would make more difficult the legal justification for the theft of their lands. All that mattered was that these particular territories somehow be usurped from the people who had settled and worked them. And so the most important thing a man or a woman can possess was stolen from the Melungeons, something far more valuable than mere land: their identity.

Another difference in how these people were treated is evidenced in the manner in which we remember and chronicle both their achievements and their suffering: for the most part, we don't. In the case of my ancestors and other Melungeons, professional historians have generally ignored them, even though they numbered in the thousands. Today their descendants undoubtedly exceed 200,000 individuals, perhaps far more, but most are unaware that they carry Melungeon blood. Amazingly, after the *Atlanta Journal-Constitution* published a story on our work on July 7, 1993, I discovered that my next door neighbor, as well as the neighbor directly across the street, were both of Melungeon descent. None of us had known of this connection until the article appeared. And this is to say nothing of the hundreds of other Atlantans that have contacted me since with similar stories.

Is it simple coincidence that in a city of three million people that I should by chance have moved into a neighborhood of Melungeons? Or is it more likely that the descendants of these early settlers are of a vastly greater number than we had previously supposed? I suggest the latter is the case, and that because of early attempts to hide such a "shameful" heritage, the true impact of the Melungeons on the Southeastern population base, and on history in general, has been grossly underestimated. Indeed, their staggering accomplishments—survival being the most astonishing of all—are seldom listed. Their race

Nancy Hopkins Kennedy,
author's mother, 1949.

Brent Kennedy,
author's father, 1947.

and prior existence having been inexplicably obliterated from the majority of even the most local of history books. But after four centuries of silent anguish, this politically convenient oversight is about to change. The truth of what happened to these people is about to be told. Not only by me, but by truly qualified researchers and, more importantly, those Melungeon descendants brave enough to stand up and be counted. People like Scott Collins of Sneedville, Tennessee, Jack Goins of Rogersville, Tennessee, and Vernoy Moore of Wise, Virginia. And those among us who still carry their names and genetic codes will, at long last, be able to honor their lives by simply being aware of their existence.

Finally, while I cannot in the space of this book touch on all facets of Melungeon history, culture, and lore, I have done my best to accurately present the more crucial facts and traits that characterize the Melungeon people. While every Melungeon family has its own set of stories (many, I am sure, more gripping than my own) I can write only of the events that shaped my particular family. It is my hope, however, that by doing a credible job of telling my story, that I will, at least indirectly, convey a sense of the history of other families as well. And, if I am fortunate, perhaps this book will serve as an emotional catalyst for others who may be ready to acknowledge and celebrate the lives of those who preceded them. If but one family finds release from a dark and painful legacy by way of what is said in these pages, then the effort will have been worthwhile.

These people, the Melungeons, are my people, and this is their story.

February 1994 and October 1996   *N. Brent Kennedy*

*Nancy Hopkins Kennedy and Richard Kennedy,
author's mother and brother, 1980.*

*"Tosh" Moore,
author's cousin, 1993.*

*Stephanie Rachel Moore,
author's cousin, 1993.*

Melungeon

The following are representative dictionary definitions.

> **melungeon,** also **malungeon** \m^{e}l^{e}nj^{e}n\ *n -s usu. cap*
> [origin unknown] : one of a group of people of mixed Indian,
> white, and Negro ancestry in the southern Appalachians esp.
> of eastern Tennessee.   —*Webster's Third New*
> *International Dictionary* (1961, 1981) 1408b

> **Me·lun·geon** (m^{e}lŭn'j^{e}n) *n.* One of a small group of dark-
> skinned people of uncertain origin living in the mountains of
> eastern Tennessee.   —*The American Heritage*
> *Dictionary of the English Language* (1981) 818b[1]

While "origin unknown" is still the most-certain conclusion, it is
variously supposed the term comes from (1) the French *mélange*,
"mixing/mixture" or "blending/blend," (2) the Greek μέλας
melas, "dark" or "black," or (3) the African-Portuguese *melungo*
or *mulango*, perhaps meaning "shipmate" (see chapter 5).

Furthermore, it may well be (4) a sixteenth-century African-Portuguese (Berber/Moorish) word meaning simply "white person"
(see chapter 6).

Finally (6), it is very interesting—and perhaps crucial—to note
that the Turkish terms *melun* and *can* (together pronounced
"melun-jun"!) are translated as "damned soul" or "one whose life
has been cursed" (see chapter 6).

---

[1]The term is lacking in *The American Heritage Dictionary* 3rd ed.
(1992).

Chapter 1

A Cry from the Grave

I lay on the examination table, the cold steel numbing my half-draped posterior, but in so much pain that a little lack of feeling was welcomed relief. Whatever I had contracted had grown progressively worse over the past several days, so much worse, in fact, that I could not walk into the hospital emergency room on my own accord. Instead, my wife had literally pulled me from the car to a waiting wheelchair and then pushed me the final few yards. Several years of puzzling exhaustion had suddenly erupted into swelling of my extremeties, painful breathing, splotched, reddened skin, aching joints and muscles, blurred vision, a searing temperature, and horrible night sweats that left me drenched. Rocky Mountain spotted fever? Lyme disease? Both of these tick-carried sicknesses were dominating the news in 1988 and, in fact, one of the nurses in the emergency room had offered this prognosis upon first seeing my mottled body.

As I lay there waiting for someone to tell me what was happening, I thought back to the recent appearance of those strange little knots on the back of my head, the uncontrollable seborreah on my scalp, face, and chest, and the fact that my normally dark, easily tanned skin remained pale and now only burned. And how my hair had gone from near black to auburn, contrasting strangely with my still dark eyebrows. I remembered the searing leg pains and accompanying mental confusion—lightheadedness and forgetfulness—that had beset me only weeks after arriving at my new administrative position at Georgetown University. The doctors there had diagnosed "sciatica" and simple stress, and I let it go at that, despite the unrelenting symptoms. I tried to rationalize why I had ignored my wife's repeated attempts to "get a good physical." I couldn't. My macho avoidance of doctors, so typical of males in general, and Appalachian men in particular, seemed on the verge of doing me in and all I could do in return was silently kick myself. Anyway, it was too late now. Something was terribly wrong, something serious, and I was consumed with the devastating possibility that my six-year-old son might grow up without a father. He deserved more.

I was fortunate that day, as I later found out, in that one of Atlanta's leading immunologists was "on call" in the emergency room. The doctor smiled, grunted a few times, and poked me here and there as he asked questions. His verdict was quick, but given my lack of medical knowledge, totally meaningless.

"The good news is that you don't have Rocky Mountain spotted fever," he said. "The bad news is that you probably have erythema nodosum sarcoidosis.[1] We don't know the cause and there's no known cure. You'll need some blood work to rule out other possibilities, and we'll probably need to do a biopsy of a lymph gland to be absolutely certain."

I had no idea of the multitude of tests and specialists that awaited me, but at that point my ignorance was a blessing. It would prove to be a grueling, painful experience best not anticipated in advance. The doctor then proceeded to share some basic information about my illness as well as a discouraging prognosis. But I needed to know more.

On crutches, my wife and I scoured the library shelves for any information on my illness. I was stunned to learn that sarcoidosis is primarily of Middle Eastern and Mediterranean disease, although it's not unknown among the Irish and some Scan-

---

[1] Erythema nodosum sarcoidosis means, literally, *red-skinned, bumpy, nodules-in-the-glands-and-elsewhere.*

dinavians as well (possibly from the documented interaction between Mediterranean/North African peoples and both the Irish and the Vikings many centuries before). And, strangely enough, it seems to be more common among both southeastern Blacks and southeastern Caucasians of seemingly unrelated ethnic backgrounds. As I would later discover, the disease is equally common among Portuguese immigrants in New England. These puzzling dispersions would turn out to be a fortuitous hint at the origin of the Melungeons. In any event, in this country the majority of sarcoid victims are Applachian whites and African-Americans, live in the Southeastern United States, and indications are that this disease, or at least the propensity toward it, is indeed genetic in nature. As I discovered several years later, some of my own ancestors suffered from symptoms of what must have been sarcoidosis as long ago as the 1860s.

Its cause unknown, sarcoidosis can be debilitating—crippling, suffocating, and even blinding its victims. A sizable percentage of the cases result in death, usually from advanced pulmonary complications. Its symptoms mimic those of crippling arthritis, lupus, tuberculosis, Lyme disease, Hodgkin's disease, glaucoma, plus searing night sweats, all rolled into one victim. And, of course, depression and mental confusion, probably stemming from the disease's attack on the brain and other internal organs. There's no known treatment, other than anti-inflammatory drugs and steroids to alleviate the pain and swelling. The victim is simply consigned to wait and see if he or she will be one of the fortunates who enter spontaneous remission (with medical evidence suggesting the more "Caucasian" the victim the more likely the chances of recovery). That was precisely my prescription: wait and see if you will live or die.

New Life

To shorten a long story, six months after that initial bout I entered into remission and my life began anew. As with others in similar circumstances, my brush with the possibility of death changed my perspective on just about everything. The grass was never greener and the sky never bluer, even on rainy days.

Nothing seemed as important or crucial as it had before, with the notable exceptions of God, family, friends, love, truth, and time, precious time to pursue those matters previously relegated to a back burner.

And with this new appreciation for time, my childhood curiosity over our origins resurfaced with a fiery zeal.

Bolstered with an unyielding determination to understand the strange etiology of my illness and its relationship to my heritage, I was compelled to take up the quest for my origins where I had so long ago left off. There were old questions that still needed answers. Questions that touched on the very essence of who my people were and are.

Why did so many members of our family have a decidedly Mediterranean appearance? Why did our ancestors migrate so readily and without apparent reason, often to and from the same general areas of North Carolina, Virginia, and West Virginia? Why did they surrender huge tracts of North Carolina land with not a penny of compensation? Why did they live on the most mountainous ridges and why had their neighbors, regardless of where they lived, invariably treated them so harshly? Why was my great-grandfather, well into this century, forcibly denied the right to vote? Had we somehow caused our own misfortune, or was it arbitrarily thrust upon us?

All these questions had previously been written off by family elders as simple bad luck, or "politics," or for this reason or for that. And, as I can even now so clearly recall, their answers nearly always were accompanied by a faraway look in their eyes, if there was any eye contact at all. I had always suspected that there was much about our family that was buried, but could never pinpoint anything specifically. The available census records yielded nothing to indicate any legal racial basis for such treatment (though prejudiced neighbors probably could have cared less about what the census records said). But back then, of course, I never had the time to pursue it. Like most folks, after a while I pretty much assumed a "What does it really matter?" attitude. But it did stick with me that we knew so little about ourselves, too little it seemed, even to a naive youngster simply curious about his heritage.

As I now know, the truth had been hidden, generation after generation: photos and family records burned time and again as each generation tried to eliminate evidence of the one that preceded it. The truth constantly altered to "protect" the generations that followed. The young and the old torn between remembering and denying one another. Like the well-meaning grandmother who, at the height of summer, dressed my mother in long sleeves, a floor-length skirt, and a broad-brimmed hat before allowing her to play outdoors—lest her skin turn "black." Just so did each succeeding generation try to protect its offspring from the equally glaring, searing rays of racial prejudice. What better way to do this than to destroy all evidence of such mistreatment? In a classic example of what sociologists term "blaming the victim," the victims—in this case, the Melungeons—eventually collaborated in the great lie, inadvertently protecting the guilty. In such a way the victims sought to escape further persecution. And they generally succeeded, though at the high cost of surrendering a significant portion of their heritage.

Out of the Melungeon Closet

As I clawed my way into the closets of our family history, I uncovered layer after layer of purposeful deceit, a veritable diary of self-imposed exile from the land of the living. We had always been on the run, dreading each door that would close in our face until we conditioned ourselves to avoid all doors, even those that might have opened. We were Melungeons, a word I had seldom heard growing up, but, as I soon learned, a word that would cut to the very heart of our problematic history.

I suppose I wasn't surprised by the revelation. As a youngster fishing at Bark Camp Lake above Stone Mountain, I had often encountered so-called "Melungeons"—usually groups of four or five men and boys tramping through the woods with antiquated shotguns. We would routinely make brief eye contact, nod, and continue on our respective ways. I knew they were "Melungeons," and considered the lowest of the low, but I was always touched by their timidity and sad eyes. And even then I thought they looked pretty much like us. Their ostracism and misery made no sense, even to a teenager. My parents could offer no rationale for it either. Too many years and too many wounds had separated us.

They and we were "free persons of color," or simply "FPC" as the early census takers had coined in shorthand. Some of us were classified as such; others (especially my family) had achieved the prized "white" classification but were still treated as FPC by their neighbors who made judgments purely on physical characteristics. And being FPC—or simply associated with FPC—was the ultimate sin, a stigma that permanently isolated its victim from the rest of so-called civilization. Neither white, black, mulatto, nor Indian, the Melungeons were left to fend for themselves, a people who were, as numerous writers have so often stated, "nobody at all."

Probably because of such scars, in the beginning I found very little enthusiasm for my search, both from within my family and without. Those within undoubtedly feared I might open a can of worms that could never be recapped, while those outside admonished me to let the past die a natural death. To let the dead lie where they are buried. To be sensitive to the "need for privacy" on the part of those who had suffered so much.

I understood the fears of those within the family. After all, such fear was the unavoidable legacy of Melungeon families. To hide our shame, as it were, we were conditioned to feel guilt over our very being, as if our mere existence was somehow an affront to common decency. I do not exaggerate. Our shame was at the most basic level—the shame of being alive. And the very real possibility of reviving that shame did give me pause about the wisdom of carrying out what I seemed determined to do.

But the concerns of those outside the circle of victims seemed more unconsciously self-serving than altruistic, although I know that most of them truly meant well. Yet somehow, since their families were not the ones who had been victimized, their advice to "just get on with life" rang hollow. They had no concept of what was at stake, of how it is impossible to "just get on with life" when one's very essence has been sucked dry. Continued silence was their only prescribed remedy.

Hearing the Cry

But centuries of such silence had made a mess of my family and untold thousands of others. I saw the still-living tentacles spawned by this morass in much of my own behavior. This silent monster still lived and breathed and it had to be confronted if we were to truly move beyond it. The restrictive choices of either quietly accepting our "stigma," or sweeping it under the rug in the pitiful self-delusion of "being like everyone else," were unacceptable. To me there seemed to be a third, admittedly blasphemous option: to embrace our heritage—whatever it might be—and wear it like a banner. So while I patiently listened to the various rationales against pursuing my heart, it was through these same arguments that I became determined to follow it.

My mother, at first uneasy over my decision to come out of the Melungeon closet, quickly came to understand. And in a simple scene that has grown more poignant with time, she sighed and said, "I suppose it's like hearing a cry from the grave, and then having to decide whether or not to answer it." She had summed it all up in one sentence. It was true. I couldn't sleep for all those cries, so many that it seemed as if the heavens had formed a weeping chorus.

But as I moved through each moment in time, adding more and more pieces to the puzzle, gathering others who hungered as I did, those unintelligible cries have evolved into booming voices. No longer weeping, but singing in loud, proud, angelic melodies. I do not know what the words are to the songs they sing, and maybe I never will. But for now, at least, I am content with the comforting knowledge that it is a *song*. The words, like all worthwhile things, will come in the fullness of time. Until that time, I just thank God for letting me hear the music.

Chapter 2

In the Beginning . . .

No one really knows when the Melungeons were first discovered, although by the time Tennessee Governor John Sevier encountered them in August 1784, their numbers were apparently substantial.[1] They lived in sizable communities primarily on the upper ridges of the eastern Tennessee counties of Hancock, Hawkins, and Rhea, in Ashe, Yancey, Surry, and Alleghany Counties in western North Carolina, and in what are now Wise, Scott, Lee, and Dickenson counties in southwestern Virginia. According to Louise Davis of the *Nashville Tennessean*, the so-called "Melungeons" were

> dark-skinned, reddish-brown complexioned people supposed to be of Moorish descent, who were neither Indian nor Negro, but had fine European features, and claimed to be Portuguese.[2]

More precisely, it was "Portyghee," as they themselves pronounced it. They claimed descent from a group of Portuguese who had either been shipwrecked or otherwise abandoned on the Atlantic coast.[3] It is important to note that, regardless of where

---

[1]Louise Davis, "The Mystery of the Melungeons," *Nashville Tennessean*, 22 September 1963, 16.

[2]Ibid.

[3]Stinson, Byron, "The Melungeons," *American History Illustrated*

the individual pockets of these people dwelled, the same Portuguese (and occasionally Turkish) origin was consistently offered to explain their existence.[4]

The term *Melungeon* itself somehow came to be associated early on with these people. It's origin and meaning unknown, most latter-day investigators have assumed the word originated from the French *mélange*, meaning "mixture." Yet the word Melungeon, pronounced as we say it today (that is, *Muh-luhn-juhn*), exists in old Spanish folk songs and usually translates as a disparaging term for a poor person or someone from a socially lower class. It is also pronounced identically to the Turkish term *melun can* and the Arabic *melun jinn*, both meaning "cursed soul" or "one whose life has been cursed."

But even if the Melungeons had indeed called themselves Melungeons when first encountering the French, there is a high probability that the French would have still referred to them as a *mélange*, because of their "mixed" physical appearance. But there is no evidence that the French ever used the term *mélange* to describe the Melungeons, despite the phonetic similarities between the two words. The evidence instead indicates that later researchers offered that possibility as a probable source of the word, and that, in reality, the term Melungeon was first associated with, or assigned to, these people by the English, not the French.

And indeed, early English explorers apparently found them in the Carolinas as early as the mid-1600s. According to Samuel C. Williams, deceased former president of the East Tennessee Historical Society, possible human remnants of Spain's early attempts at colonization were living in a mining community in the southern Alleghenies in 1654.[5] Williams also described an exploratory journey made in April 1673 by James Needham, an

---

(November 1973): 41.

[4]Swan Burnett, "A Note on the Melungeons," *American Anthropologist* (October 1889): 347.

[5]Samuel C. Williams, *Early Travels in the Tennessee Country* (Johnson City TN: The Watauga Press, 1928) 29-30.

Englishman, and Gabriel Arthur, possibly an indentured servant, along with eight Indians, to the Tennessee Valley. A portion of Needham's account of this trek is fascinating and relevant enough to be included here.

> Eight days journey down this river, lives a white people which have long beards and whiskers and weares clothing, and on some of ye other rivers lives a hairy people. Not many yeares since ye Tomahittans sent twenty men laden with beavor to ye white people: they killed tenn of them and put ye other tenn in irons, two of which tenn escaped and one of them came with one of my men to my plantation. As ye will understand after a small time of rest one of my men returns with his horse, ye Appomatock Indian and twelve Tomahittans, eight men and foure women. One of these eight is hee which hath been a prisoner of ye white people . . . ye prisoner relates that ye white people have a bell which is six foot over which they ring morning and evening and att that time a great number of people congregate togather and talkes he knowes not what.[6]

Jean Patterson Bible, in her excellent resource book *Melungeons: Yesterday and Today*, when commenting upon this same passage, notes the seeming Latin influence in the tolling of the bell and congregation of people.[7] Another early Melungeon historian, Bonnie Ball, in *The Melungeons*, adds her same interpretation based on the reported tradition that these people would also bow in the direction of the bell.[8] The mere existence of a bell at that time period would seem to indicate a Catholic origin. And the fact that these English-speaking Indians did not understand the language of these mysterious, apparent Europeans is also an intriguing piece of evidence. These "hairy people" worshipping at a bell were obviously not English.

Despite this early evidence of a Latin influence, by the 1750s—when the first great waves of English and Scotch-Irish

---

[6]Ibid, 28-29.

[7]Jean Patterson Bible, *Melungeons: Yesterday and Today* (Rogersville TN: East Tennessee Printing Co., 1975) 94.

[8]Bonnie Ball, *The Melungeons*, 8th ed. (Big Stone Gap VA: privately printed, ©1991).

settlers came down the Valley of Virginia—the Melungeons were speaking a broken form of Elizabethan (that is, sixteenth-century) English and carrying English surnames as well. And yet, no matter how distant their settlements lay from one another, they invariably claimed to be Portuguese, or occasionally Spanish or Turkish. One can only imagine the perplexity experienced by the exhausted Scotch-Irish as they encountered these improbably dark-skinned mountaineers, speaking broken English, claiming a Mediterranean heritage, placing southern European cupolas over the graves of their dead, sporting English surnames, practicing Christianity, and—most frustrating of all—dwelling on the very land for which the Scotch-Irish had just crossed the ocean. Supposedly open land, promised them by the King of England no less. It must have been an immense disappointment and, in their defense, for several years they did try to work around the problem. They settled elsewhere, on this knoll instead of in that valley, or on that ridge rather than in that meadow. But as their numbers grew, the patience of the equally disadvantaged "Ulstermen" correspondingly dwindled. Finally, a consensus was reached: the Melungeons had to go.

Welcome to the Census

At first it was through sheer intimidation, even occasional violence, with no thought given to pulling the weight of the law in behind them. But as time went on, the nominally civilized Scotch-Irish contrived to change the racial classification law itself. The first U.S. censuses in the 1790s were to be proving grounds for stripping the Melungeons of their properties and their rights. Faced with an inability to classify the Melungeons into any of the then four available legal categories (White, Indian, Negro, or Mulatto), the Scotch-Irish cleverly deployed a new term: "free persons of color," and used it to strip the Melungeons of their lands, their right to be represented in court, their right to vote, and their right to public education. One sweep of the judicial pen—the simple arbitrary assignment of the letters "FPC" (or "FC" to which it was sometimes shortened) alongside one's name in the federal census—and, presto!, you became a legally disenfranchised person. And no amount of begging, wailing, or gnashing of teeth could save you after such a pronouncement.

When the Melungeons countered that they were "Portyghee," and thus fellow Europeans who should be immune to such a law, the Scotch-Irish countered with scoffing mockery backed up by overwhelming firepower. "FPC" soon gave way to "mulatto" as census takers lost patience with those Melungeons seeking to hold on to their lands. On several of the old census records one can see the term "Port." crossed through and "mulatto" written in its stead. We can only imagine the arguing at the census taker's desk that led to such an abrupt, on-the-spot change of status.

The varying physical types within the same families only added to the complexity of the census taker's job. While most had darker complexions, a few possessed an alabaster hue with fair, even blond hair, and many, if not most, of the very darkest had both light blue eyes and extremely aquiline features. A sizable number exhibited the unusual combination of red hair, blue eyes, angular facial features, and skin the color of fresh mud. And by the early 1800s some were indeed true "mulattos," with marriage between browbeaten classes not only increasingly unavoidable but desirable under the circumstances. Over time, the Melungeons truly became an ethnic brew with an increasingly foggy cultural memory.

In any event, census takers eventually settled in on the terms "FPC," "FC," or "mulatto" to describe any person of darker complexion, regardless of their ethnic origin. Native Americans were eventually lumped into the "mulatto" class, forever skewing the work of later genealogists. In fact, as we will later see, many census takers—including the registrar of vital statistics for Virginia well into the 1940s—would arbitrarily divide people into but two races: "white," which meant only "pure" northern Europeans, or "black," which meant blacks, mulattos, Indians, Jews, Arabs, Asians, and so forth, or anyone with as much as one-sixteenth so-called "nonwhite" (that is, non-Anglo) blood. Intended to make the Appalachian census taker's task a simpler one, this narrow classification must have made for an absolute nightmare.

One can easily envision the census taker's growing impatience as he tried to patiently deal with troublesome folk who just did not play by the racial rules. And it is also easy to see how unreliable the federal censuses from this time period are when trying to determine an individual's true ethnic makeup.

Dr. Horace Rice expounds on the inevitable cultural horrors wrought by such rigid interpretations of race in his thorough exploration of a Virginia mixed-race Indian people known as the "Buffalo Ridge Cherokees." These are a people with an obviously heavy Indian component who received a legal governmental mandate that—because there is some "black" component in their gene pool—they cannot be Indian![9]

A human being can be of many ethnic heritages, *and indeed all human beings are just such a mixture*. To arbitrarily assign a single "ethnic" label to anyone based simply on skin color is asinine, and the result is a Hitler-like interpretation of "us" and "them." Those who take at face value the racial designation of the early census takers are themselves being taken. It may appear laughably stupid, but this is precisely the sort of legalized labelling that occurred from the very first U.S. census. And it did not go over very well with those who happened to possess a variety of heritages.

To be expected, the taking of censuses became a dreaded occasion for both the Melungeons and the census takers. And, as one might also expect, the Melungeons eventually and inevitably sought to avoid censuses altogether. This had the unfortunate result of rendering large portions of the Melungeon population officially nonexistent, leading future historians to seriously underestimate their numbers. Our ancestors' understandable avoidance of censuses would also seriously frustrate future family genealogists. It would seem to the descendants of these first families that our grandparents had indeed crawled out of

---

[9]Horace R., Rice, *The Buffalo Ridge Cherokee: The Colors and Culture of a Virginia Indian Community* (Madison Heights VA: BRC Books, 1991). [Address: BRC Books, P.O. Box 1018, Madison Heights VA 24572.]

the earth, with no evidence of being propagated in the usual biological fashion—which was pretty much the argument the Anglos had always made.

From that point onward, the Melungeons became officially a mixture of White, Indian, and Black, or in the reputed words of one nineteenth-century Tennessee senator, a "Portuguese nigger."[10] And although most Melungeons had always disclaimed any appreciable Native American heritage, they, along with their likely cousins, the North Carolina "Lumbee" Indians, would later be legally categorized as "Croatan Indians" in the belief that they might represent a remnant of the Lost Colony. While such names as "White," and "Dare" are common among the Lumbees and, to a lesser degree among the Melungeons, only the Lumbees readily embraced the official designation of "Indian." Most of the Melungeons held out, never taking advantage of this classification. Instead, they continued in their struggle to preserve their Old World customs while insisting on their southern Europeanism or Turkish roots. Nevertheless, by 1834 Melungeons had been stripped of most rights of citizenship in both Tennessee and North Carolina. Their final retreat to the least desirable pinnacles of the forbidding mountain ranges followed shortly thereafter. The rest, as they say, is history.

The Melungeon Marauders

But don't assume the Melungeons went to their fates quietly. They didn't. Many fought, and many died in defending what they knew in their souls to belong to them. The Civil War presented them with a unique opportunity for vengeance. Bands of Melungeon men formed what came to be known as the "Melungeon Marauders," spreading terror throughout East Tennessee and, to a lesser extent, Southwest Virginia. My own family, mostly Mullinses, Nashes, Osbornes, and Halls, engaged in such chicanery, leading of course to even greater prejudices against them after the war. Now the white community's previously

---

[10]Will Allen Dromgoole, "The Melungeons," *The Arena* 3 (1891): 472-73.

simple prejudice escalated to include an accompanying terror of these dark-complexioned people. Just as thousands of years earlier Roman mothers would control unruly children with the admonition, "Hannibal is at the gates!," so did Appalachia's Anglo mothers tell their own misbehaving offspring, "Be good, or the Melungeons will get you!"[11]

In the end, however, their numbers were too few to "get" anyone, and the whole world it seemed was out to get them. One by one, family by family, they retreated off the prime lands they had settled, moving farther and farther up the slopes of the towering Appalachians. Newman's Ridge in Hancock County, Tennessee, the Blackwater area of Lee County, Virginia, Stone Mountain in Wise County, Virginia, and Caney Ridge in Dickenson County, Virginia, became four of the better-known mountain refuges, but certainly not the only ones, for these defeated people. Hundreds, if not thousands, migrated westward in the mid-1800s, mostly to Arkansas, Oklahoma, Texas, and California. Others made their way to Maryland and Ohio. But a few, typically those with fairer skins, managed to hold on to their Appalachian bottomlands. They even prospered. It was these "lucky" few who most quickly lost their roots and whose descendants are only now beginning to find themselves.

Melungeon Lore—Unfortunate but Colorful

No background discussion on the Melungeons would be complete without mentioning a few of the better-known "characters." The public fascination with some of our progenitors—especially those who learned how to survive through more creative, usually illegal, activities, deserve special mention.

Probably the best-known Melungeon was a nineteenth-century giant of a woman named Mahala Mullins. Mahala, or "Big Haley" as she was known, was born Mahala Collins in the 1830s, but married a Melungeon relative of mine with the surname of Mullins. She lived in a cabin perched high atop a nearly

[11]Edward T. Price, "The Melungeons: A Mixed Blood Strain of the Southern Appalachians," *The Geographical Review* 41 (April 1951).

Mahala Mullins with jar of moonshine, ca. 1870. Courtesy Scott Collins.

inaccessible peak on Newman's Ridge above Sneedville, Tennessee. Best known for her size (probably in excess of five hundred pounds) and her moonshining (when you are Melungeon there are not a lot of employment opportunities available), "Big Haley" remains arguably the most famous of all Melungeons.

The amusing quote most often associated with Mahala Mullins were the words of one young deputy who tried to arrest her for selling her illegal brew, but discovered he couldn't get Mahala through the narrow doorway of her mountain home. Explaining to the judge the reason for Mahala's absence from the courtroom, the deputy said, apparently straight-faced, "She's ketchable, but not fetchable."

While Mahala's life was far more complex and productive than this single incident would indicate, this isolated, rather sad event has nevertheless come to epitomize her life. Mahala was dealt a double dose of inequity: first, because of her color she never quite fit into life as defined by the whites, and second, because of her size, at death she likewise did not fit into the standard available caskets. She was instead buried in a makeshift coffin built around her bed, then awkwardly carried through a wall opening made by knocking out part of the stone chimney. The men bore her body into the woods several hundred feet from her house and there, alone and in the middle of nowhere, Mahala Mullins was laid to rest. Forgotten by most folks over the years, her grave was only recently rediscovered by a group of searchers including a descendant, Hancock County's Clerk and Master Scott Collins. Scott, a key member of our Melungeon Research Committee, and his companions found Mahala's marker buried under a foot of soil and entangled in the roots of a mammoth tree that still gives shelter to her disintegrating bones.

Mahala was indirectly immortalized by popular Kentucky novelist Jesse Stuart. Stuart wrote the sometimes wearisome but always compelling *Daughter of the Legend*, the tragic story of a Wise County, Virginia white boy's ill-fated marriage to a beau-

Arched windows, typically Melungeon.
(Mahala Mullins's house, front.)

tiful East Tennessee Melungeon girl. Stuart's oversized, kindly character, "Sylvania," was without doubt based on Mahala "Big Haley" Mullins of Hancock County, Tennessee.

Mary Polly Collins Cox.
Courtesy Willie R. Mullins, Sr.

The second most famous Melungeon, also a resident of Newman's Ridge and another ancestor of Scott Collins, was the eighteenth-century patriarch Vardeman Collins, sometimes called "Vardy" or "Navarrh" Collins. It was for Vardeman that the "Vardy School" for Melungeon children in Hancock County, Tennessee was named (about 1910). No longer in service, the old, whitewashed Vardy School sits empty on a hillside in Vardy, slowly giving in to the weathering of time and the elements.

A local schoolteacher, Mary Rankin, dedicated her life to teaching Melungeon children at Vardy and is remembered with great reverence by the Melungeon people. Ironically, in the early 1980s I lived in the Rankin House on the campus of Tusculum College in Greeneville, Tennessee, the very house where Mary Rankin grew up. My son was born in Greeneville and came home to the Rankin House. None of us was aware of the history of the home that housed us.

Anyway, it is certain that Jesse Stuart was familiar with the legends of Mahala Mullins and Vardy Collins. After a single visit to the Tennessee ridge these Melungeon forebears called home, I reread *Daughter of the Legend* and discovered a ferocious realism that totally escaped me on my first

Scott Collins and longtime Sneedville resident Huie Mullins.

reading. Stuart's Sylvania was undeniably Mahala, and Mahala combines both the heroic and the tragic elements that make a rare few of us unforgettable.

Andrew Jackson "Brandy Jack" Mullins. Courtesy Ginger Senter.

Arguably the third most famous, or infamous, Melungeon was actually an entire family—the Mullinses of southwestern Virginia. This nineteenth-century clan, primarily "Brandy Jack" Mullins and his uncle "Counterfeitin' Sol" Mullins, were renowned for their silver-working and, more specifically, their exquisite counterfeiting of so-called "Spanish-milled dollars." Both were eventually caught, with Brandy Jack spending significant time in prison for fraud. There were certainly other Melungeon counterfeiters, and many, many expert metal-workers, but this particular family seems to have garnered the most press. They're also my direct ancestors, which has created for them a special place in my heart and provided some personal spark to what has sometimes been a pretty tedious search for roots.

Reinventing Oneself

Rediscovering one's heritage is not an exact science, and ossified family tangles are not easy to untangle. To accurately tell the story of the Melungeons means also telling the story of those with whom they interacted and intermarried. And it means separating fact from fiction, legacy from legend, and sorting through page after page of erroneous and even fabricated genealogies. In the pages that follow, I have tried to do just that, but such a task has demanded much genealogical "reading between the lines." I have had to question so much that has been "written in stone" by my forebears, and handed down from generation to generation. But hints at the truth come from the changing "facts" surrounding certain ancestors, sometimes reflected in a single individual who was "Portuguese" at birth, "Portuguese-Indian" as an adult, and, at death, simply "Indian." And then, three generations later, remembered variously as French, "Black Dutch," Scotch-Irish, or English!

It hasn't been easy, and in some cases rather painful: informing sincere family members that their cherished genealogical charts are riddled with bogus ancestries, most the result of this or that well-meaning ancestor's pitiful attempts at survival, has not always endeared me to others. But, indeed, the truth will set us free. Hopefully that same truth, belatedly recognized, will set free my ancestors as well. And while we may not always be able to say with certainty that something is indeed true, it can still be helpful to at least learn what is not true.

The truth of my family, inasmuch as we know it, is in the pages that follow. And while it is not always pleasant to recount, the freedom gained by doing so makes the telling immeasurably worthwhile.

Chapter 3

No Place to Hide
Part 1. Momma's Side

William Roberson II (1789–1880), my great-great-great-great-grandfather, practically settled Wise County, Virginia. And while he was not the very first settler to push his way into those forbidding mountains, he certainly found a great deal of elbow room when he arrived in the early 1800s via nearby Russell County. He became a substantial landholder, a respected politician, and the ancestor of many of the region's outstanding leaders. No local history book is complete without telling of the exploits and accomplishments of William Roberson, and giving a photograph of his striking and somewhat brooding countenance.

The history of his father, William Roberson I (1758–1847), prior to arriving in Wise County is, in a word, confusing. William I's own statements serve to muddy the genealogical waters. He claimed to be of Scotch-Irish descent, to have been born in London, England, and to have served in the Revolutionary War, being variously credited with either six years or eighteen months of service, depending on who was recording the story. Yet he had neither documentary evidence of having served nor witnesses who could substantiate that service.[1]

William Roberson II

Sometimes it was said that the family was actually of French descent. William Roberson himself said that he came to this country in 1778, or 1773, depending on the document one reads. He said he had enlisted in the Continental Army at Greenbrier County, Virginia (now West Virginia), but his widow said he had joined in Charleston, South Carolina. While there is no doubt that William Roberson actually did serve in some capacity for

---

[1]Pension record of William Roberson, no. W 2668, transcript of personal appearance before the County Court, Sevier County, Tennessee, 3 September 1832. National Archives, Washington DC.

some length of time during the Revolutionary War (records indicate he enlisted as a private in the Continental Army in 1780), his descendants have endured untold challenges in trying to make sense of this service and, quite frankly, the whole portion of his life prior to his arrival in Wise County. There is a reason for that, as you have no doubt by now guessed: William Roberson was either himself Melungeon, conceivably borrowing at least a portion of his heritage from another "William Robertson," or, perhaps more likely, had married a Melungeon or mixed-race wife. If the latter scenario is correct, this would have brought down upon his head the usual prejudices that forced such mixed couples to continually move and reinvent their "roots." Once one begins the weaving of a fabricated heritage, the opportunities for misstatements and "lapses of memory" multiply accordingly. All the signs are there with William I.

Roberson Line

William Roberson + Delilah Ritchie
(1758–1847)   (?)
William Roberson II + Hannah Hutchinson
(1789–1880)   (1787–?)
Mary Polly Roberson + Alexander Hall
(1816–1858)   (1816–1866)
Louisa Hall + Wickliff Nash
(1844–1916)   (1840–1897)
Floyd Ashworth Nash + Margaret "Maggie" Bennett
(1882–1922)   (1888–1965)
Rexie Nash + William Sylvester "Taylor" Hopkins
(1906–1933)   (1899–1986)
Nancy Hopkins + Brent Kennedy
(1929–)   (1928–)
N. Brent Kennedy
(1950–)

William Sr.'s first wife, and the mother of most of his children, was Delilah Ritchie, probably the daughter of Crockett Ritchie. Crocket Ritchie had always claimed to be English, but it is very possible that either he or his wife Susan Grigsby, or possibly both, were North Carolina Melungeons or other mixed-heritage individuals. Whether either parent carried Melungeon genes, their children tended to marry into Melungeon families, usually a sign of relatedness.

Indeed, Crocket's son John Ritchie married Sylvania Sizemore, daughter of the self-proclaimed Cherokee Edward "Ned" Sizemore, born in 1725.[2] (At least the records indicate that Ned's descendants stated that Ned claimed such a heritage. This may have been their attempt to validate tribal membership.) Nearly two thousand of Ned Sizemore's descendants have sought enrollment in the Cherokee Nation on the basis of their belief that Ned was, as he supposedly claimed, a Cherokee. In fact, so many Sizemore descendants have made such a claim that there is a separate Sizemore file at the tribal office in Cherokee, North Carolina. Most, if not all of these petitions have been denied. The reason, of course, is that Ned Sizemore, if he was Indian at all, had south-central Virginia (and possibly Melungeon) roots versus western Carolina (and Cherokee) roots.

Ned most likely was born in Virginia and then migrated south across the North Carolina border where he eventually met up with other Melungeon families. There is, in fact, stronger support that Ned's wife was either a Virginia Indian (possibly one of the Algonquian tribes) or even Melungeon, and that much of the Sizemore claim to Native American heritage can more easily be ascribed to her. The fact his daughter sported the common Melungeon given name Sylvania, the pseudonym Jesse Stuart hung on the Mahala Mullins character in *Daughter of the Legend*, while admittedly only circumstantial, is at least interesting.

Another of Crockett Ritchie's sons, James, married a dark-skinned, North Carolina woman whose maiden name was Keith. Keith just happens to be a known North Carolina Melungeon surname. This woman, despite her dark skin, was not an Indian and, in fact, was frightened to death by all Indians, friend or foe,

---

[2]Jean Ritchie, *Singing Family of the Cumberlands* (Lexington: University of Kentucky Press, 1988) 99.

because her first husband had been murdered by one in her presence. So while it is possible that Crockett Ritchie was English, his children did seem to gravitate toward mates with darker complexions. Delilia Ritchie may have been no different than her siblings in her attraction to William Roberson I.

William Roberson's second wife, Nancy Breden Shepard, in her 1833 claim for bounty land from the state of Tennessee, stated that her husband had been born in Scotland, although William Roberson I had claimed an English birth. He further claimed to have come to Sevier County, Tennessee from a previous stopover in Greenbrier County, West Virginia. His son William Roberson II generally claimed to have been born in Greenbrier County, although some family members feel there is a case for a Jonesboro, Tennessee birth site.

What is not in contention, however, is the fact that William I lived at least part of his early years in Greenbrier County and this fact adds additional credence to the hypothesis of a Melungeon-related heritage. Greenbrier County, as we now know, was an eighteenth-century destination site for North Carolina Melungeons and other mixed-race groups seeking to escape the growing pressure of land-hungry Anglo immigrants. In fact, the Melungeons pretty much settled Greenbrier County in the early 1700s. That William Roberson I lived there at that particular time period is interesting, to say the least. That he left Greenbrier County at the same time the Melungeons were being "evicted" is even more intriguing.

Of related interest is the Roberson surname itself. First, there was apparently no agreement among the family members themselves as to how to spell the family name, a strange phenomenon for an Anglo family immigrating to an Anglo-dominated country. "Roberson," "Robertson," "Robinson," and "Robeson" all pop up as surname spellings for various branches of the family. Surely, if William Sr. really did come from England, Scotland, or Ireland, he would have known how to spell his last name. Or at least early on have settled in on one spelling and taught that spelling to his children. A family tradition says that the children of William Roberson II and his second wife Matilda Roan Vanover changed their surname to

"Robinson" to differentiate between themselves and the children of the first marriage. This could be true, but does not explain the incidences of other spellings prior to and following this purported event. Of some curiosity, too, is William I's own admitted early meanderings in southern North Carolina and South Carolina, undoubtedly placing him within the geographical region of North Carolina known as "Robeson" county. Could William I have "borrowed" his surname from the name of the county, or from early settlers for whom the county was later named?

Is it pure coincidence that Robeson County, North Carolina is home to the mysterious Lumbee Indians, a dark-skinned, mixed-heritage population who, in the mid 1800s, were also called Melungeons? But then there is also the fact that the first land grant made in Greenbrier County, West Virginia, on 26 April 1745, and consisting of 100,000 acres, was made to "John Robinson et al."[3] John Robinson was the treasurer of colonial Virginia and would certainly have been a well known name to any of the state's residents, especially those in Greenbrier County. If William Roberson had been a relative of John Robinson, it is unlikely that he and his family would have left such vast holdings to begin scratching out new lives in Wise County. Could William I have borrowed his surname from this famous Virginian? Any of these scenarios are plausible, but the reality of the matter is that we may never know with certainty the precise origins of William Roberson.

What did William Sr. look like? His widow described him as "five foot high, blue eyes, black hair." This tells us little, but we do have a firsthand observance of some of Roberson's children and grandchildren as related by a neighbor born in 1849:

The Robinsons [sic] were rich people who lived at Castlewood. They were dark and said to be Portuguese.[4]

---

[3]Ruth Woods Dayton, *Greenbrier Pioneers and Their Homes* (Charleston: West Virginia Pub. Co., 1942) 16 (repr.: Education Foundation, Inc., Charleston WV, by C. J. Krehbiel Co., Cincinnati, 1977).

[4]Priscilla Harding, 24 August 1942 statement to Elihu Jasper Sutherland, as reported in *Pioneer Recollections of Southwest Virginia*

It is an interesting ethnicity for reputed Englishmen to claim, and the alleged Portuguese heritage—for the offspring of *either* of William Sr.'s marriages—is one that has been consistently overlooked or discounted by later family researchers.

William Roberson II moved with his father to Russell County, Virginia where he married Hannah Hutchinson (1787–?), the daughter of Peter Hutchinson and Nancy Green. Nancy was very likely part Powhatan Indian, Green being one of the more common Powhatan-related surnames. Peter Hutchinson, who was born in Carrickfergus, Ireland in 1748, met and married Nancy in Culpepper, Virginia, the heart of Monacan and Algonquin country. His sister Elizabeth Hutchinson Jackson was the mother of President Andrew Jackson. It is not known how close Peter was to his presidential nephew. One thing is known, however: Andrew Jackson would later engineer the removal of the Cherokees via the infamous "Trail of Tears" and many Melungeons would also be caught up in that mass deportation. Maybe this is why they came to think of themselves as Cherokees. Even today I receive letters from Melungeon kinfolk in Oklahoma who made their way westward with the Cherokees in 1834.

It is also quite likely that old Andy Jackson knowingly shipped off some of his own relatives to the western territories. It is interesting that our family has not clung as tightly to the memory of Andrew Jackson as one might expect relatives of an American president to do. It is especially interesting when one realizes that, since Jackson had no natural children of his own, the descendants of Peter Hutchinson—Melungeons!—would likely comprise the closest living relatives to this former president. It is a seemingly disjointed thought, although we shouldn't overlook Jackson's own seemingly out-of-character adoption of an orphaned Indian boy that he apparently loved very dearly. If the Melungeons and Andrew Jackson shared any common philosophical ground at all, it would have been their mutual dislike of the English. Jackson, being Scotch-Irish, had been terribly abused

(Clintwood VA: Mullins Printing, 1984) 169. [Address: Mullins Printing, Rt. 2, Box 307, Clintwood VA 24228.]

by the English. One officer, in fact, struck the adolescent Jackson with a sword, nearly killing him.[5]

A Melungeon President?

Speaking of presidents, research team member Eloy Gallegos has discovered that there is a good deal of circumstantial evidence that Abraham Lincoln shared a Melungeon heritage, possibly through both parents. Swarthy, with central Virginia and Cumberland Gap roots, as well as an established familial penchant for hiding their genealogy, Lincoln's family fits the Melungeon mold extraordinarily well. Lincoln's paternal grandfather, also named Abraham Lincoln, emigrated with his wife Bathsheba Herring and their five children from Rockingham County, Virginia to Kentucky in the early 1780s. Why would an established settler leave the beautiful Shenandoah Valley for the wild, untamed lands of Indian-dominated Kentucky? History has recorded that Lincoln's grandfather was able to sell his Virginia properties and buy unlimited Kentucky properties for forty cents an acre.[6] Perhaps that was the reason. Or perhaps the Lincolns were simply part of the late-eighteenth-century Melungeon migration westward. We know little of Bathsheba Herring, but we do know that their children tended to exhibit dark features, including President Lincoln's father Thomas Lincoln.

> As Tom Lincoln came to full growth, he was about five feet, nine inches tall, weighing about 185 pounds. . . . His dark eyes looked out from a round face, from under coarse black hair.[7]

Historian Philip van Doren Stern agrees with the accuracy of this description of Thomas Lincoln, stating that Thomas Lincoln "had dark hair and complexion, and so did his son."[8] And who

---

[5]Robert V. Remini, *The Life of Andrew Jackson* (New York: Penquin Books, 1990) 8.

[6]Carl Sandburg, *Abraham Lincoln: The Prairie Years*, vol. 1 (New York: Harcourt, Brace & World, 1926) 4-5.

[7]Sandburg, *Abraham Lincoln: The Prairie Years*, 1:6-7.

[8]Stern, *The Life and Writings of Abraham Lincoln*, Modern Library

did Thomas Lincoln marry? Why, the mysterious Nancy Hanks, of course, known to all American schoolchildren as the president's devoted but enigmatic mother.

Nancy Hanks was born in Virginia in 1784, and traveled as a baby via the Cumberland Gap to Kentucky. Nancy's mother Lucy Hanks, nineteen at the time, brought Nancy to Kentucky alone, the unknown father remaining in Virginia. While history has not recorded the identity of Nancy's father, it has documented that Lucy's sister and Nancy's aunt—also called Nancy Hanks—married Virginian/Kentuckian Levi Hall around the year 1802. Who was Levi Hall? He was probably a member of the sizable Hall family of southwestern Virginia and eastern Kentucky—my family, in fact. Our Halls migrated in significant numbers from central Virginia to western North Carolina and, in the late 1700s, up into southwest Virginia and across the border into Kentucky. The name "Levi" has been associated with our Halls for generations, a more recent one being the Levi Hall who lived near the Kentucky-Virginia border in the early part of this century.[9] Another Levi Hall was the son of Andrew Hall of Russell County, Virginia, a relative of my Halls, Isham and Alexander.[10] In any event, it would appear quite likely that the Levi Hall that married President Lincoln's great-aunt was a member of our family and probably a Melungeon. And this possibility, if true, would indicate early on a propensity on the part of Lincoln's ancestors to associate with and even marry so-called "mixed-blood" people.

While we know that President Lincoln's father displayed some non-Anglo physical characteristics, what about Nancy Hanks herself? Carl Sandburg presents this appraisal of her appearance:

> Her dark skin, dark brown hair, keen little gray eyes, outstanding forehead, somewhat accented chin and cheek-bones, body of slender build, weighing about 130 pounds—these

---

(New York: Random House, 1940) 8.

[9]Sutherland, *Pioneer Recollections of Southwest Virginia*, 224.

[10]Ibid., 108.

formed the outward shape of a woman carrying something strange and cherished along her ways of life.[11]

And President Lincoln's self-description:

If any personal description of me is thought desirable, it may be said that I am, in height, six feet four inches, nearly; lean in flesh, weighing on the average one hundred and eighty pounds; dark complexion, with coarse black hair and grey eyes. No other marks or brands recollected.[12]

Abraham Lincoln was always uncomfortable with his appearance, knowing that his physical characteristics, to say nothing of his lanky build, stood out in stark contrast to his fairer-skinned peers. And he was equally aware of the differences between his and their family backgrounds. From childhood there had been the typical Melungeon tendency to hide one's past.

While young Abe was growing up, he heard his father and John and Dennis Hanks tell neighbors this and that about their families, what kind of men and women they had for relatives, kinfolk, blood connections. And young Abe learned there were things the Lincolns and Hankses didn't care to tell the neighbors concerning Abe's mother Nancy and his grandmother Lucy.[13]

Some of this may have had to do with grandmother Lucy Hanks having been named a "loose woman" by a Kentucky grand jury in 1789, her daughter Lucy being born out of wedlock.[14] And yet, if Lucy's father was a Melungeon or other "mixed-race" person, this may have been her only social recourse—that is, bearing the stigma of being a loose woman as opposed to marrying a persona non grata. Indeed, most of the courts of that time would not have permitted such a marriage anyway. Perhaps, if this scenario is true, Lucy simply opted for the lesser of two evils. Certainly

---

[11]*Abraham Lincoln: The Prairie Years*, 1:13.
[12]Gerald Sanders, *Abraham Lincoln Fact Book* (New York: Eastern Acorn Press, Publishing Center for Cultural Resources, 1940) 31.
[13]Sandburg, *Abraham Lincoln: The Prairie Years*, 1:56.
[14]Ibid., 1:58-59.

the physical traits of the resultant child, Nancy Hanks, would indicate a non-Anglo father. Of equal interest is that when Lucy Hanks did marry, it was to one Henry Sparrow. Sparrow is *not* a typical Anglo name. It is, however, a quite common Indian name, especially among the aforementioned Buffalo Ridge Cherokees.[15] And, as we will see later, there was definite admixture between these central Virginia Indians and the Melungeons. Coincidence perhaps, but when combined with the other circumstantial evidence, a strong case for a "mixed-blood"—and possibly Melungeon—heritage for our sixteenth president.

Whatever the truth, one is forced to at least consider the strong probability that the rigors associated with a mixed-race ancestry may have created in Abraham Lincoln an individual sensitive to the plight of those who looked different. And, ironically but fittingly, this painful background may have contributed to the evenutal moral stand that transformed this particular president into an American, and even a global, icon.

The Melungeon-Cherokee Link:
Benge, Bunch, Gist, and Sequoya

As we now know, being Cherokee was far preferable to being Melungeon, especially when the government later began paying restitution to displaced tribal members. It is interesting that most Melungeon families have legends of Indian blood—usually Cherokee—"way back" somewhere, but very few can prove it. I have turned over every possible stone attempting to do so.

This is not to say the Cherokees and the Melungeons had no interlinkings. They did. Micajah (or "Micager") Bunch, a nineteenth-century Melungeon, often called the "king of the Melungeons," took a Cherokee bride. Even today, there are numerous Cherokees in western North Carolina with the surnames of Bunch, Bench, Hall, Martin, French, and Goins.

---

[15]Horace R., Rice, *The Buffalo Ridge Cherokee: The Colors and Culture of a Virginia Indian Community* (Madison Heights VA: BRC Books, 1991) 36 and 47.

I have a strong suspicion, for which I have no evidence, that the infamous eighteenth-century Cherokee warrior Chief Benge, also known as Captain Bob Bench, was more Melungeon than Cherokee. Benge, who was eventually ambushed and scalped by white settlers near present-day Norton, Virginia, has always been something of a mystery, even to the Cherokees who made him a chief. For one thing, some historians have thought him to be Shawnee, while others have posited that he was half-Cherokee and half-Irish. Still others have supposed that he was simply a renegade white man with an unusually dark complexion. One thing is for certain, despite his dark complexion, Benge had reddish-auburn hair and blue eyes, the same characteristics possessed by a large number of Tennessee Melungeons.

Another Cherokee mystery has focused around the renowned Sequoya, inventor of the Cherokee alphabet. Sequoya, also known as George Gist (purportedly the son of the famous backwoods frontiersman Christopher Gist, and an alleged Cherokee wife he later deserted), was also recognized for his silver-working abilities. How did Sequoya, and other Cherokees as well, learn this complicated, typically Melungeon craft? My family genealogy provides a hint at the source of Sequoya's skill. One of my direct ancestors, Benjamin Bowling (1734–1832), was a Melungeon and a close friend of Christopher Gist. Bowling's wife Patsy Phelps was also a Virginia Melungeon and her mother was believed to have been a Gibson (see Bowling genealogical line later in this chapter). Our family oral history says that Benjamin and Patsy introduced Gist to his wife, a cousin of Patsy's, thus indicating that quite possibly Sequoya's mother was at least partially, if not totally, Melungeon.

Even more intriguing, there is evidence that Christopher Gist was himself partly Melungeon mixed race. Charles A. Johnson discusses the mystery of Christopher Gist's background. Although supposedly a native of Maryland, in Johnson's own words, "the early life of Christopher Gist is obscure."[16] What is

---

[16]Charles A. Johnson, *Wise County, Virginia* (Johnson City TN: The Overmountain Press, 1938).

intriguing, however, is his acknowledged close relationship with the Cherokees, his residence in the heavily Melungeon Yadkin River area of North Carolina, and his verified friendship with known Melungeons. Additionally, he left a widow, his second wife Judith, whose maiden name was Bell, or Belle, a common Melungeon surname, and his own physical characteristics are suggestive of a Melungeon, as opposed to his purported German, background. In 1793, General James Taylor in an unpublished autobiography described Gist as follows:

> I found him alone in a large military marquee [tent] with his servants, I think about thirty or forty, about the fire. He was a large man of dark complexion and I think near six feet high, and of a commanding and intelligent appearance.

Hopefully, some qualified historian will find these possibilities intriguing enough to pursue.

More on the Robersons, Greens, Halls, and Mullins

Nancy Green, Peter Hutchinson's wife, was the daughter of Lewis Green who fought in the Revolution and was a close friend of Daniel Boone. Lewis was supposedly a cousin to Nathaniel Green of Revolutionary War fame, but this cannot be verified. There is the strong possibility that Lewis Green's wife, Susan, was either an Indian or a Melungeon, but we will probably never know with any degree of certainty. We do know that Green is a common surname among the Powhatan and Pamunkey Indians, and, as we will see later, these particular tribes do play an integral role in Melungeon history. But for the time being, all we can say with indisputable confidence is that their daughter Hannah Hutchinson and her husband William Roberson II produced handsome, dark-complexioned children, including my great-great-great-grandmother Mary "Polly" Roberson (1816–1868).

English, Indian, Portuguese, or a combination thereof, Mary "Polly" Roberson married my great-great-great-grandfather Alexander Hall (1816–1866), whose Melungeon heritage is not in question. "Alex" Hall's father, Isham Hall II (1785–1856), also claimed to be from Greenbrier County, Virginia, but moved early on to North Carolina. It was without doubt a return home after things in West Virginia did not work out. Isham's wife, a Melungeon woman named Jane Mullins, was born in North Carolina.

This continuing Greenbrier County connection among various lines of our family is of great historical interest for several reasons. First, because Greenbrier County is contiguous to Virginia's New River Valley, a favorite northward migration route of early North Carolina Melungeons seeking new lands to replace those stolen from them, and second, because it is but a short distance south from the Phillipi and Chestnut Ridge area of Barbour County, West Virginia, home of another mysterious, dark-skinned Appalachian people known as the "Guineas."

The "Guineas" of West Virginia

The Guineas have a history nearly identical to the Melungeons, are physically indistinguishable from them, and, remarkably, even carry many of the same surnames: Collins, Adams, Miner, and Kennedy, to name just a few. Yet, interestingly enough, apparently few if any anthropologists have ever formally suggested a genealogical link between the two populations. Even Hu Maxwell's rather lengthy and heavily detailed history of Barbour County makes no mention of the Guineas, and little mention of any residents with a Guinea surname, except one "Richard Male" who built a cabin in the late 1700s.[17]

Interestingly, Maxwell also says that as of 1899 there were no Indians left in Barbour County, this in spite of the Guineas' long-standing claim to be Indian[18]. Given their tragic notoriety, one can only assume that Maxwell consciously excluded them from his remarks, just as the Melungeons were also generally excluded from their related regional history books. After a tele-

---

[17]Hu Maxwell, *The History of Barbour County, West Virginia.* (Parson WV: McClain Printing Co., 1968) 192 (repr. from 1899 edition by Acme Publishing Company, Morgantown WV).

[18]Ibid, 25.

phone call to a so-called "Guinea" in Phillipi, West Virginia—a Kennedy, in fact—and discovering that we are almost certainly related, I no longer doubt that the Guineas and the Melungeons share a common heritage.

In my opinion, the Guineas were simply those family members who, in the mid- to late-1700s, migrated northward from Greenbrier County as opposed to our ancestors who returned "home," or at least southward. Both groups had started out as the same eighteenth-century families exiting central Virginia and North Carolina under the increasing pressure of Scotch-Irish and English encroachment. Later intermarriages with non-Melungeon families undoubtedly introduced into the Guineas such surnames as Croston, Dalton, Mayle (Male), and Pritchard. Amazingly, Library of Congress ethnologist William Gilbert recorded that the Guineas have a tradition of Portuguese intermarriage, primarily with the "Mayle" or "Male" families. Also, according to Gilbert, there has been a persistent theory tying the Guineas to the Spaniards, "perhaps some lost followers of DeSoto."[19]

The term "Guinea" does not come from a "West African" origin, as postulated by some, but rather from the popular English coins by the same name circulated in this country during and following that pre-Revolution era. The English Guinea, equivalent to twenty-one shillings and used in this country up to, and even after, the Revolutionary War, was a targeted coin of Melungeon counterfeiters. The manner in which the nickname "Guinea" came to be associated with the West Virginia Melungeons was probably neither as exotic nor originally as derogatory (at least this was the intent of those who offered these theories) as prior writers and researchers would have us believe. It only became an intentionally abusive term when later Anglo settlers needed an African-sounding name to justify their tyranny over these people. And to those seeking a purely African explanation

---

[19]William Harlen Gilbert, Jr., "Mixed Bloods of the Upper Monongahela Valley, West Virginia," *Journal of the Washington Academy of Sciences* 36/1 (15 January 1946): 11.

for the presence of the "Guineas," the existence of the West African nation of Guinea seemed the perfect link.

Even though genuine African Guineas did indeed arrive on our shores in the 1700s, I have been unable to establish any linkage whatsoever between these two peoples. The ancestors of the West Virginia Guineas, in fact, already resided in North Carolina and Virginia prior to the arrival of the African Guineas. And while there is undoubtedly an African component within at least some of the Melungeons (and probably a West African one), the irony is that it played no role in giving the "Guineas" of West Virginia their pseudonym. As this book is being completed, I continue to work with my West Virginia cousins in establishing as much as we possibly can about how the Melungeons came to be in Barbour County.

The "Black Nashes" of Coeburn Mountain

Nash homestead on Coeburn Mountain, ca. 1910.

Back south in Virginia, Isham Hall II's son Alexander Hall, like many Melungeons, was given the opportunity to fight for the Confederacy. He rose to the rank of Captain and served under General Stonewall Jackson before returning home to his previous inferior status. The Confederacy desperately needed soldiers and, much as today, young men with intelligence and ability would, regardless of their color, be given a chance to die on the battlefield.

Louisa Hall Nash, ca. 1866, author's great-great-grandmother.

Alexander Hall's son-in-law Wickliff Hendricks Nash (1840–1897), himself part Melungeon, would also serve with the Confederacy, rising to corporal in the 48th Virginia Infantry, Company B, before being demoted to private for some unknown misbehavior.

"Wick" Nash had inherited the fairer features of his father William Nash III (1801–1876), and not the darker ones exhibited by his Melungeon mother Margaret Ramey (1804–?). William III's marriage to Miss Ramey had not set well with William Nash, Jr. (?–1825) and his wife Margaret Hendricks, well-to-do settlers at New Garden (Lebanon), Virginia. The Nashes may possibly have been Welsh, or they may have been Melungeon related. William Nash I and his wife Sarah, in fact, supposedly lived and died in England, and William Jr. supposedly migrated to this country around 1775. This remains conjecture, with no documented evidence to either support or disprove its verity. Either way, old William Jr.

was not a happy man when William III married a Melungeon girl, or so the story goes. When he learned that the deed had been done and was too far gone to alter, he threw down the fine top hat he was wearing and stomped it flat. While his action had no appreciable influence on the marriage, so far as we know, it no doubt exerted an irreparable effect on the hat.

William III and Margaret Ramey thus produced "Wick" Nash and Wick married Alexander Hall's and Mary "Polly" Roberson's beautiful, dark-skinned daughter Louisa (1844–1915). It is safe to say, while many Melungeon women may have equalled Louisa's beauty, none surpassed it. She was a prize catch and, while, given his fairer features, Wick might have left Wise County and escaped the Melungeon cycle, he didn't. He was too taken with Louisa and Louisa was not about to leave her family. Melungeons had survived by being clannish and one did not cut off family that easily. Family, unlike land, was forever, and throughout her later life Louisa demonstrated her emotional attachment to this defining Melungeon sentiment. But not being able to marry locally, possibly because of Wick's fairer complexion, they crossed the border into Catlettsburg, Kentucky to complete the matrimonial act. This is oral tradition, with some evidence indicating that they "remarried" later in Virginia.

Nash Line

William Nash I + Sarah (?)
(lived and died in England)
William Nash Jr. + Margaret Hendricks
(?–1825)   (?)
William Nash III + Margaret Ramey
(1801–1876)   (1804– ?)
Wickliff Nash + Louisa Hall
(1840–1897)   (1844–1916)
Floyd Ashworth Nash + Margaret "Maggie" Bennett
(1882–1922)   (1888–1965)
Rexie Nash + William Sylvester "Taylor" Hopkins
(1906–1933)   (1899–1986)

Nancy Hopkins + Brent Kennedy
(1929–)   (1928–)
N.Brent Kennedy
(1950–)

Hall—Mullins Line

Isham Hall + Mary Mullins
(?)   (?)
Isham Hall II + Jane Mullins
(1785–1856)   (1799–?)
Alexander Hall + Mary Polly Roberson
(1816–1866)   (1816–1858)
Louisa Hall + Wickliff Nash
(1844–1916)   (1840–1897)
Floyd Ashworth Nash + Margaret "Maggie" Bell Bennett
(1882–1922)   (1888–1965)
Rexie Nash + William Sylvester "Taylor" Hopkins
(1906–1933)   (1899–1986)
Nancy Hopkins + Brent Kennedy
(1929–)   (1928–)
N. Brent Kennedy
(1950–)

Regardless, Kentucky was a popular marrying ground for so-called "mixed" marriages, at least in the mid 1800s. It was wilder country and the authorities were not so harsh in their enforcement of antimiscegenation laws. The southeastern counties of Harlan, Letcher, Floyd, and Pike also proved to be attractive to young Melungeons seeking new lives. Many of my own family, especially Mullinses, Halls, Kennedys (some of whom changed

Louisa Hall Nash and daughters, ca. 1910.

their spelling to Cannaday), Nashes, and Hopkins migrated in heavy numbers into Kentucky.

Louisa Hall Nash's handsome and ambitious brother Floyd Hall likewise left Wise County to try his luck in Kentucky. Her less dark but still Mediterranean-looking brother succeeded beyond the levels any Melungeon could hope for, becoming an outstanding lawyer, accumulating large land holdings and the respect of his fellow Kentuckians. Given the chance, Melungeons could do anything their fairer-skinned neighbors could. Given their drive, I would say even better. Tellingly, in Floyd Hall's abbreviated memoirs as included in a local history book by Mabel Green Condon entitled *The History of Harlan County, Kentucky* (date of publishing unknown), he weaves a tale of noble French ancestry, something his descendants—including myself— grabbed hold of to explain our darker features. He himself may well have believed it; certainly those of us who followed did. And in fairness, it may not have been totally incorrect since, as we will later see, some French undoubtedly did intermarry with the Melungeons.

Canara Nash, author's
great-uncle, ca. 1910.

Albert Nash and
Helen Bennett Nash.

Louisa Hall and Wick Nash had thirteen children, six girls
and seven boys, one of whom, handsome and dark-skinned Floyd
Ashworth Nash, was my great-grandfather. Louisa also had
adopted a homeless boy, a ten-year-old black child working in a
Coeburn feedstore, and given him the family surname. "Charlie"
Nash was reared along with the others and, years after he had
grown and left the area, he would return as often as possible to
pay his respects to Louisa, the only mother he had ever known.
The Nashes had been called the "Black Nashes" well before the
adoption of Charlie, but his addition to the family further fueled
the local fires of racism. White people just did not do things like
that, or at least not in those days. In the viewpoint of townfolk,
the Nashes were just asking for trouble. I often wonder where
Charlie's descendants are today, and what tales and stories have
been passed to his progeny. There are so many broken circles
waiting to be completed.

Floyd Nash and his six brothers learned early on that to survive as a Melungeon you had to be tough. Granted, his father
had built his mother a fine house on Coeburn Mountain, but it

was some five miles away from town. The top of Coeburn Mountain became a sort of "halfway house" for Melungeons intent on
clawing their way out of misery. Stone Mountain, only a few
miles above the "plateau" of Coeburn Mountain, remained Wise
County's version of Newman's Ridge— inaccessible, undesirable
land ceded to the Melungeons in exchange for prime property
they had originally held. The more level land where the town of
Wise now sits, or the beautiful farm country of the Powell Valley
were territories well worth stealing. No one cared about Stone
Mountain.

*Aaron "Pat" Nash, son of
Louisa and Wicklief Nash.*

*Rexie Nash Hopkins,
ca. 1925.*

The Nashes managed to hold on to the semiflat land east of
Wise and running right to the edge of the mountain where one
can now look over and see the town of Coeburn far below.
William Nash III had once owned some 6,000 acres of land, but
according to family legend had "gambled it away," or simply engaged in stupid business practices. My personal speculation is
that much of it was probably taken, albeit "legally," after his
marriage to Margaret Ramey. Most of it today lies within the
federal government's extensive Jefferson National Forest. But to

cover the truth the family had to turn William III into an irresponsible reprobate who squandered the family fortune. All that was left was the still significant 500 acres he somehow held on to for his children, probably—and ironically—by placing the title in his wife's name. While William may well have ended his life as an irrational alcoholic, there were plenty of coconspirators who helped him along his way.

Nash Vengeance

Being limited landowners and having a fine home, of course, did not insulate the Nashes from the prejudices of the townfolk. Merchants sometimes refused to sell to them, they couldn't attend school, and they couldn't vote, or at least were forcibly prevented from doing so until the present century. Occasionally these inequities and other slights got to be too much, and Louisa's sons would take a small measure of vengeance here and there.

Consider the time one of the Nash girls became pregnant and the fair-skinned town boy who had contributed to her condition refused to marry her. In her shame she left Coeburn Mountain to birth the baby elsewhere. Her brothers were infuriated and knew they could not let such an inequity pass lest other injustices be visited upon them. So one afternoon as the guilty party and his brothers rode their horses down a familiar trail, the Nash brothers, sitting atop their own mounts, waited for them. No one will ever know what actually transpired on that trail, but the offending brothers died there, apparently killed in a hellacious shoot-out. A subsequent trial sent brother Floyd to prison, but, given the lack of firm evidence, he was released two years later. As far as is known, there were no repeats of such incidents. A statement on the seriousness of Nash vengeance had been made.

Dark-Skinned Cowboys

Well into the 1900s, the Nashes and Halls were not permitted to vote. Great-grandpa Floyd, his brothers Emory, Canara, and Trig (and possibly brothers William, Aaron Patrick,

Lilbourne, Bob, and Albert), as well as some of the Hall boys, would take a measure of vengeance on their oppressors. They would strap on their guns, mount up on horseback, and move down the winding mountain trail to Coeburn, where invariably word of their impending arrival had preceded them. There they would ride through the deserted streets, devoid of inhabitants, eerily silent, gloating in the tremors that must have been running down the spines of their terrified antagonists. Sometimes they

Floyd and Maggie Bennett Nash,
with Baby "Beau" Nash, ca. 1905.

would fire their weapons at whatever struck their fancy; at other times they would simply parade about. They must have made quite a sight, those dark-skinned cowboys, riding silently but determinedly into a town that didn't want them.

Some years later, an older Floyd would again ride into Coeburn—this time alone—to vote. He tied up his horse and walked toward the polls, only to find his way blocked by a town tough. A fight ensued. Floyd was badly beaten but won and continued his walk to the polls, only to be blocked by a larger line of unyielding townsmen. In what must have been a defining moment of his life, Floyd drew his gun and fired several bullets at his tormentors' feet, then watched this paper tiger of a crowd scatter. A Melungeon voted in Coeburn, Virginia that day. But the victory was not savored for long. Sometime later, in his own front yard, Floyd Nash was shot for refusing to sell a pint of moonshine to a town passerby. A week later, just entering the fortieth year of his life, he died an agonizing death from blood poisoning resulting from the improperly treated wound.

Louisa the Peacemaker

Louisa Hall Nash, ca. 1910.

It wasn't surprising that townspeople were scared of the Nashes. Word had been sent by Wick to the local sheriff to stay away from his place. When there was reason to make an official call on the Nash homestead, permission was usually asked first, and the visit was often made to Louisa rather than the boys. Louisa was tough as nails, but easier to talk to. After all, she wanted a peaceful life for her family more than anything else.

The advisability of working through Louisa could certainly be verified by one neophyte deputy who tried to serve a warrant, possibly for shooting firearms over the weekend in the town of Coeburn. Though his intent had been to arrest one of the offenders, he was quickly disarmed and forced to climb a big tree— backwards. Such a feat required unusual dexterity—placing one's back and buttocks against the trunk, then stretching the arms awkwardly backwards to grasp the tree, and finally pushing oneself upwards by digging one's feet and heels into the bark. Not an easy assignment when the tree was tall, thick, and covered with barnacle-like bark. But the Nash boys could do it unscathed and it would be good fun to see if the milky complexioned town boy could do it as well. He could not, of course. And after his unsavory ordeal was over, he left

Coeburn Mountain much chagrined and with a raw and bloody back as well. No warrant was served and no follow-up visit was made. Sometime later, a deal was made providing that no law officer would set foot on Nash land until he got clearance from Louisa. This set well with Louisa and was certainly a lot less painful for the lawmen.

Louisa Hall Nash was known not only as a peacemaker, but as the consummate mountain hostess. In those days before motels dotted the mountain landscape, weary travelers—mostly Melungeons, but all peaceful people were welcome—would stop off at Louisa's place for a hot meal, conversation, and a dry place to spend the night. And no charge ever, for anything. It was Louisa's heritage, the traditional looking after one's fellow human beings. Although most of her family living today never knew her, we all feel that we did. The wonderful things she did as a matter of course continue to live on, and that's the way good works should be.

One relative does remember her, although the memories are a bit misty, given their formation around 1915. One of my great aunts, Evelyn Stallard Smith, recalls her grandmother Louisa and several of Louisa's female relatives regularly walking from the homeplace the half-mile or so up to Evelyn's home:

> What I remember most is that they were always dressed in black. Long black dresses that covered them from neck to wrist to ankle. I never saw them in anything else.

Also of interest, many of my aunts recall that, despite the matriarchal nature of our family, when walking the women always followed the men by several yards. Our women may have been strong and certainly ruled the roost at home, but when traversing the countryside they kept to the rear. My mother echoes a similar memory at family picnics, a memory of little boys being extra special. While she and her female cousins, most often Shirley Skeen Moore, would be assigned the task of swatting flies away from the food, the same-aged boys were left unencumbered, playing to their hearts' content. There's no doubt that, even today, while our female cousins are dearly loved and cared for, both our women and men have a special place in their hearts for the boys. It is an interesting familial characteristic, given the strength and beauty of our women.

Bennetts, Brass Ankles, Lumbees, and Redbones

When Great-grandfather Floyd died, he left behind eleven children, nine girls and two boys. He also left behind a wife, a Melungeon girl from North Carolina named Margaret Belle Bennett. "Maggie," as she was known, was the daughter of Spencer Bennett and Dicie Mullins, both from Yancey County, North Carolina. Spencer's parents, John Bennett and Elizabeth Adkins, were married in 1854 at the age of eighteen. Spencer was described by those who knew him as a short, slightly built man with a very dark complexion. He often wore a little beret, and family members remember him alternately claiming either French or "Black Dutch" descent. "Black Dutch," "Black German," and "French" were highly popular "code names" for eighteenth-century Melungeons. The same families who had claimed to be Portuguese in the 1700s suddenly became "Black Dutch" or "French" in the 1800s. Again, it was better to be "French" or "Black Dutch" than to be Melungeon, and by the early 1800s "Portuguese" had become synonymous, at least for the census takers, with "Melungeon."

As intimated earlier, there may indeed have been some French component among the Melungeons. In the 1730s a group of French Acadians escaped from their English captors in South Carolina and disappeared into the Appalachians. Although a few made their way to Canada, most were never heard from again, and it is quite possible that at least some of them may have been taken in by the Melungeons. And, as we will see still later, there are other, even more fascinating theories on how the so-called "French" component may have entered the theoretical Melungeon milieu. Regardless, people soon figured out this name game, and in some parts of the region the term "French" became synonomous with Melungeon. Ironically, or perhaps it was planned, the surname "French" itself made its way into both the Melungeon and Cherokee populations, which complicated the use of "French" as an ethnic origin.

William "Bacon Bill" Mullins, William's son Noah,
and Noah's son Friend. Courtesy Bill and Betty Belcher.

Actually, the Bennetts may not have been typical western North Carolina Melungeons, but members of a related group variously called the Siouans, or Croatan Indians or, more recently, the Lumbees. This mysterious mixed-race group, concentrated today in the southeastern North Carolina county of Robeson and the northeastern South Carolina counties of Marlboro, Dillon, Marion, and Horry, claims descent from surviving members of Sir Walter Raleigh's "Lost Colony" of Roanoke

"Black Ira" Mullins family. Pound, Virginia.
(Ira was William "Bacon Bill's" son.)

Island who intermarried with Native Americans. First encountered in 1709 by Englishman John Lawson as he traversed
through the Carolinas, the Lumbees even then seemed different
than other southeastern Indians. Lawson referred to these people—now called Lumbees—as "Hatteras Indians," and reported
their own legend of non-Indian ancestors from the coastal area
of North Carolina. Among the more common family names of the
Lumbees are Berry, Brooks, Chavis, Cumbo (according to family

legend to be "of Portuguese extraction"[20]), Dare, Lucas, Martin, Locklear, Oxendine, White, and, last but not least, Bennett.

The Lumbee story is fascinating and has spawned a number of books well worth the reading, the most recent by the Lumbee historian Adolph Dial, professor at Pembroke State University in Pembroke, North Carolina.[21] Historian Theda Perdue of the University of Kentucky also provides excellent and quick background reading on the Lumbees and other North Carolina Indians in her 1988 booklet *Native Carolinians.*[22]

Adkins—Bennett Line

Wilson Adkins + ? Stacey
(?)   (?)
Sarah Adkins + John Bennett
(John was apparently from Robeson County, N.C.)
John Bennett Jr. + Elizabeth Adkins
(left N.C. during early 1830s)
Spencer Bennett + Dicie Mullins
(married in Kentucky, 1876)
Margaret "Maggie" Bennett + Floyd Ashworth Nash
(1888–1965)   (1882–1922)
Rexie Nash + William Sylvester "Taylor" Hopkins
(1906–1933)   (1899–1986)
Nancy Hopkins + Brent Kennedy
(1929–)   (1928–)
N. Brent Kennedy
(1950–)

Whether John Bennett Jr. was a Melungeon or a Lumbee, his wife Elizabeth was most likely a member of the Melungeon

---

[20]Douglas L. Rights, *The American Indian In North Carolina.* (Winston-Salem NC: John F. Blair, Publisher, 1957) 146.

[21]Adolph L. Dial, *The Lumbee*, Indians of North America series, ed. Frank W. Porter III (New York: Chelsea House Publishers, 1993).

[22]Theda Perdue, *Native Carolinians: The Indians of North Carolina* (Raleigh: North Carolina Department of Natural Resources, 1988).

"Adkins" clan that populated Ashe and Yancey counties. John's mother Sarah was supposedly an Adkins as well, although we cannot be certain of that at this late date. In any event, Sarah and husband John Bennett left North Carolina with their children in the late 1830s, about the time that North Carolina declared Melungeons to be "free persons of color." They were headed for new land and new hope in southwestern Virginia. And while they undoubtedly knew the Mullinses prior to leaving North Carolina, it was in Virginia where the two families became one.

Maggie Bennett's mother Dicey Mullins was the daughter of William "Bacon Bill" Mullins (1818–1914) and Sarah Ann Rose (1829–?). Sarah Ann's family had come from the Toe River/Rock Creek area in North Carolina, and were descended from John Rose. William's parents were David "Spotted Dave" Mullins and Virginia "Jane" Short. Dave was a North Carolina Melungeon while Jane Short's family, although originally North Carolinians, were Floyd County, Kentucky Melungeons. Dave's father, Booker Mullins, supposedly from Franklin County, Virginia, was the progenitor of many later Melungeons in Virginia, Kentucky, and Tennessee. Booker's wife, Nancy Stanley, was the daughter of North Carolina Melungeons William Stanley and Nancy Mullins. Aside from William, Dave's other children included Wilson Mullins (1824–1892), into whose family Mahala Collins (later "Big Haley" Mullins) married, and Polly Anna Mullins who eventually married her cousin, the infamous Melungeon counterfeiter Andrew Jackson "Brandy Jack" Mullins.

Mullins-Stanley-Short-Rose Line 1

William Mullins + Elizabeth (?)
(?) (?)
Booker Mullins + Judith (or Nancy) Stanley
(1762–1864)   (?) (possibly two marriages)
"Spotted" Dave Mullins + Virginia "Jane" Short
(1798–?)   (1807–?)
William "Bacon Bill" Mullins + Sarah Anne Rose
(1818–1914)   (1829–?)

Dicie Mullins + Spencer Bennett
(Married in Kentucky, 1876)
Margaret "Maggie" Bennett + Floyd Ashworth Nash
(1888–1965)   (1881–1922)
Rexie Nash + Taylor Hopkins
(1906–1933)   (1899–1986)
Nancy Hopkins + Brent Kennedy
(1929–)   (1928–)
N. Brent Kennedy
(1950–)

Stanley-Mullins-Short-Rose Line 2

William Stanley + Nancy Mullins
(?)   (?)
Judith (Nancy) Stanley + Booker Mullins
(?)   (1762–1864)
"Spotted" Dave Mullins + Virginia "Jane" Short
(1798–?)   (1807–?)
William "Bacon Bill" Mullins + Sarah Anne Rose
(1818–1914)   (1829–?)
Dicie Mullins + Spencer Bennett
(Married in 1876)
Margaret "Maggie" Bennett + Floyd Ashworth Nash
(1888–1965)   (1882–1922)
Rexie Nash + William Sylvester "Taylor" Hopkins
(1906–1933)   (1899–1986)
Nancy Hopkins + Brent Kennedy
(1929–)   (1928–)
N. Brent Kennedy
(1950–)

Brandy Jack was Polly Anna's first cousin by means of both the direct Short connection (Brandy Jack's mother Ann Short was a sister of Polly Anna's mother), as well as the Short family's own descent from Booker Mullins. Old Booker may have had a previous marriage, possibly before his marriage to Nancy

Stanley. The name Judith Bunch, or Bench, has occasionally been tied to Booker, but I have been unable to produce any documents directly indicating a matrimonial link. It would be interesting, however, since the surname "Bunch" is a common surname among the South Carolina "mixed blood" Indian tribe known as the "Brass Ankles." And, as mentioned earlier, "Bench" is a well-known Cherokee surname. The Brass Ankles, in turn, have been linked to the "Croatan" (that is, Lumbee) Indians across the border in South Carolina

"Crippled Basil" (l) and "Little Andy" (r) Mullins. Courtesy Pictureman Mullins.

and, given many shared Melungeon surnames, both of these Carolina tribes undoubtedly share at least a partially common heritage with the Melungeon people.

Brandy Jack Mullins and Polly Anna Mullins were my great-great-great-grandparents, thus infusing a quadruple dose of old Booker's genes into my countenance. Such close marriages were not uncommon among Melungeons, given the cohesiveness of the families and the unavailability of alternative spouses. Frankly, it is amazing there were not more such marriages than there were. In any event, it guaranteed that those of us who followed would better preserve our genetic heritage than one might normally expect. While a negative from the viewpoint of reproductive science (and from a personal basis as well), it is probably an advantageous occurrence to those pursuing the genetic origins of our people. And we certainly have an advantage in maintaining physical family traits. It seems there is always a trade-off.

Mullins-Stanley Line

William Mullins + Elizabeth (?)
(?)   (?)
Booker Mullins + Judith (or Nancy) Stanley
(1762–1864)   (?) (possibly two marriages)
Sherwood Mullins + Mary Polly Roberts
(1790–1881)   (1800–?)
Sherod Mullins + Anne Short
(Anne is a sister to Virginia "Jane" Short)
(Sherod is a brother to "Spotted" Dave Mullins)
Andrew Jackson "Brandy Jack" Mullins + Polly Anna Mullins
(1824–1917)   (1838–1864)
W. S. Powers + Lucinda Mullins
(?)   (1859–?)
David Kennedy + Ida Powers
(1880–1959)   (1884–1903)
Napoleon B. Kennedy + Tessie Colley
(1903–1986)   (1899–1988)
Brent Kennedy + Nancy Hopkins
(1928–)   (1929–)
N. Brent Kennedy
(1950–)

Stanley-Mullins Line

William Stanley + Nancy Mullins
(?)   (?)
Booker Mullins + Nancy (or Judith) Stanley
(1762–1864)   (possibly two marriages)
"Spotted" Dave Mullins + Virginia "Jane" Short
(1798–?)   (1807–?)
(Jane was a sister to Anne Short)
("Spotted" Dave is a brother to Sherod Mullins)
Andrew Jackson "Brandy Jack" Mullins + Polly Anna Mullins
(1824–1917)   (1838–1864)
W. S. Powers + Lucinda Mullins
(?)   (1859–?)

David Kennedy + Ida Powers
(1880–1959)   (1884–1903)
Napoleon B. Kennedy + Tessie Colley
(1903–1986)   (1899–1988)

The Legacy of Maggie Bennett Nash

After Floyd Nash's untimely death, Maggie Bennett Nash did the best she could in raising eleven children. She refused offers of adoption and somehow scrounged a living out of her farm on Coeburn Mountain. By this time some of Floyd's brothers had left the area for such faraway places as Duluth, Minnesota, Arkansas, Ohio, Georgia, and northern Kentucky, seeking anything better than what Wise County had to offer. Maggie was left there to bear a disproportionate share of the dark Nash legacy and how she reared her children is still something of a miracle. She planted crops and the children helped tend them. She raised chickens, and grapes, and blackberries which I can still see hanging from the long demolished grape arbors that Floyd had so carefully constructed. In the summer, the thick growth of vines made Granny's little vineyard a jungled fantasy land. The big sheltering oak under which we would gather to picnic, the always-full rain barrel at one corner of the house, the consistently ripe walnut tree whose nuts would almost permanently stain our prying little fingers, the hand-drawn water well at the end of the well-worn wood walk, the "two-seater" outhouse, and the rusted farm implements that had once been gripped by Floyd's strong hands, now stashed in a dark corner of the barn, made Granny's humble home too special for words. I will never be able to adequately convey the emotions attached to that little plot of land. No longer standing, I miss Granny's house almost as much—but not quite—as I miss her.

Like many other destitute mountain people, Granny made what little spending money she could from the sale of produce to the Coeburn hospital and moonshine to the Coeburn men. Most of our family today do not know this, but will once they read this book. Some will be ashamed and will wonder why I am telling such a terrible secret. I am not ashamed. I am proud of Granny for not giving up, for having the will and the courage to do whatever it took to survive. This is the same Granny who, for months after John F. Kennedy's assassination, would collapse into tears each time his face would appear on her crackling little black-and-white television set. The same Granny who stalwartly gathered her frightened grandchildren about her when the northern lights unexpectedly catapulted across the night skies, and, trusting the Lord, waited for His hand of judgement to rapture them to some better place.

Moonshining was not what Granny wanted to do, just as it was not what Big Haley Mullins on Newman's Ridge wanted to do. But what else was there for a Melungeon widow with a wagon load of children? So she took what life had begrudged her and made the best of it.

Sorrows and Tribulations

But that life was not easy either, with a seemingly endless stream of tribulations lined up outside Granny's door. She lost a son, Emory, to a drunken fool who shot him for looking at his girlfriend. Emory—they called him "Bo"—died in the arms of his father's sister, Aunt Mary Nash, who happened to be working at the Coeburn Hospital when they carried him in. And there were other losses as well. According to those who knew her, my grandmother Rexie Nash was a strikingly beautiful woman. Typically Melungeon. Men would sneak second glances as she walked by, striving to catch one more glimpse of her dark beauty. But most would only look or make dirty jokes as she passed. After all, to most white folks, a pretty Melungeon girl was just something to look at, to admire from a distance. Never touch one since you might catch something dark and mysterious. Or if you did touch her, deny it later. But not every man felt this way. One man liked what he saw and let her know straight on that he had a hankering for her.

William Sylvester Hopkins, or "Taylor" as everyone knew him, quickly set his sights on marrying Rexie Nash. Taylor hated the name Sylvester, but it was a family name handed down for generations. "Taylor" fit him better: tall, black-haired, dark-complexioned, an immaculate dresser. And adventurous. At sixteen he had lied about his age and joined the army to fight Pancho Villa along the Texas-Mexico border. Later he shipped off to France to fight the Germans in World War I. He survived both conflicts, but despite seeing the world, had come back to settle in Wise. Taylor Hopkins was half Melungeon himself, but *his* family had made it into town. By the time he met Rexie, in the 1920s, the Hopkins had a thriving grocery business and were on the verge of entering social acceptance. Their success probably looked good to Rexie, too. A way of getting off the mountain.

The Hopkins of Kentucky

The Hopkins had originally come out of North Carolina, but by way of a two-generation stopover in eastern Kentucky. Taylor's father King Solomon Hopkins was one-half Melungeon, "Sol's" daddy "Preacher John" Hopkins having married a Melungeon girl named Hannah Osborne. Hannah's daddy Cornelius Osborne had moved to Pike County, Kentucky from Virginia along with his father Sherwood Osborne. Sherwood's parents were Solomon Osborne (1765–?) and Hannah Bowling (1766–1850). Cornelius, like so many others in the family, had been born in Rowan County, North Carolina, moved north to New River, Virginia, and finally ended up on top of isolated Cumberland Mountain, near the Virginia-Kentucky border. Hannah Osborne was probably born on Cumberland Mountain, and it was somewhere around the mountain where she met "Preacher John" Hopkins, her future husband. One of their babies they tagged with a good biblical name, King Solomon Hopkins.

"King Sol" grew up to be a giant of a man, so tall and strong for his day—six feet, four inches and well in excess of two hundred pounds—that nobody much bothered him. If you are determined to be born a Melungeon, it doesn't hurt to be born a very large and strong Melungeon. King Sol' was my great-grandfather and is still something of a legend in the family.

Hopkins Line

William Hopkins + Rosanne Phillips (Phipps)
(?)   (?)
"Preacher" John Hopkins + Hannah Osborne
(?)   (?)
King Solomon Hopkins + Elvira "Vie" Swindall
(?)   (?)
William Sylvester "Taylor" Hopkins + Rexie Nash
(1899–1986)   (1906–1933)
Nancy Hopkins + Brent Kennedy
(1929–)   (1928–)
N. Brent Kennedy
(1950–)

Osborne Line

Enoch Osborne + Jane Hash
Solomon Osborne + Hannah Bowling
(1765–1852)   (?)
Sherwood Osborne + Louisa (Levicy) Collier
(1788–1838)   (?)
Cornelius Osborne + Rhonda Hammond
(?)   (?) (m. 1850)
"Preacher" John Hopkins + Hannah Osborne
(?)   (?)
King Solomon Hopkins + Elvira "Vie" Swindall
(1878–1952)   (1879–1951)
William Sylvester "Taylor" Hopkins + Rexie Nash
(1899–1986)   (1906–1933)
Nancy Hopkins + Brent Kennedy
(1929–)   (1928–)
Brent Kennedy
(1950–)

Bowling Line

Benjamin Bowling + Patsy Phelps
(1734–1832)   (Patsy's mother was supposedly a Gibson)
Hannah Bowling + Solomon Osborne
(1766–?)   (1768–?)
Sherwood Osborne + Louisa (Levicy) Collier
(1788–1838)   (?)
Cornelius Osborne + Rhonda Hammond
(?)   (?)
"Preacher" John Hopkins + Hannah Osborne
(?)   (?)
King Solomon Hopkins + Elvira "Vie" Swindall
(1878–1952)   (1879–1951)
William Sylvester "Taylor" Hopkins + Rexie Nash
(1899–1986)   (1906–1933)
Nancy Hopkins + Brent Kennedy
(1929–)   (1928–)
Brent Kennedy
(1950–)

Sol' married a part-Melungeon like himself, a pretty, raven-haired, black-eyed girl named "Vie" Swindall. Her father John Wesley Swindall (1826–1900) had served in the Union Army, and was either one-half or one-fourth Melungeon, his maternal grandfather being Simon Tolliver, one of the "Black Tollivers" of Ashe County, North Carolina. And, in reality, although John carried the surname Swindall, there is a strong probability he was either a Tolliver or a Phipps. His mother Elizabeth Swindall gave him her surname, the father's having been lost to posterity, except for the century-and-a-half rumor that either Solomon Tolliver (son of Simon Tolliver) or a Phipps had been his father.

John Wesley Swindall, like so many other Melungeons, had also moved from Ashe County, North Carolina to New River, Virginia before finally ending up near the Kentucky-Virginia border. It was in Kentucky where he joined the 39th Kentucky Regiment and rose to the rank of sergeant.

John Wesley, as he was referred to, married Polly Phipps (1835–1907), more than half Melungeon and likely a cousin. Polly's father Joseph Phipps (1797–1840) had left Ashe County, North Carolina with his supposedly Cherokee bride Patsy White (1800–1856), a daughter of another supposed Indian named Bob White, who also lived in Ashe County, but had apparently moved there from farther south. Like Spencer Bennett, Bob White was probably Lumbee Indian, the "White" surname being quite common among the Lumbees. Joseph Phipp's parents were Sam Phipps (1762–1854) and Betty Reeves (1765–1845). Sam's father, Joseph Phipps, Sr. (1730–?) supposedly married one of Ned Sizemore's daughters, her name unfortunately lost to history, which meant that Sam was probably also part Melungeon. His wife Betty Reeves was almost certainly Melungeon, the daughter of Ashe Countians George Reeves, Sr. and Jane Burton. As Mary Killen Hollyfield, a descendant of Betty Reeves recalled in 1929:

> The Reeves are said to have come from Portugal. They had brown eyes and black hair. I've heard it said they were part Indian too.[23]

Betty Reeves herself claimed to be "Portuguese Indian," a term used by many Melungeons to explain their heritage. The "Portuguese" portion of the term was eventually dropped, most likely because (1) no one believed it, (2) the Melungeons had no proof to back it up, and (3) it had become synonymous with "Melungeon" anyway. Being "Indian" was increasingly considered preferable to "Melungeon" or "Portuguese." Regardless, all this meant that John Wesley Swindall's wife Polly Phipps was probably more than half Melungeon/Indian and that her daughter Vie, adding John Wesley's genes, was about the same. The children of Vie and King Solomon Hopkins, including my grandfather Taylor, consequently ended up at about one-half of whatever a nineteenth-century Melungeon was.

---

[23]Ibid., 174: Mary Killen Hollyfield personal statement, 22 May 1929.

White Line

Bob White + ?
(?)   (?)
Patty White + Joseph Phipps
(1806–1858)   (1797–1840)
Mary Polly Phipps + John Wesley Swindall (Phipps/Tolliver)
(1835–1907)   (1826–1900)
Elvira "Vie" Swindall + King Solomon Hopkins
(1879–1951)   (1878–1952)
William Sylvester "Taylor" Hopkins + Rexie Nash
(1899–1986)   (1906–1933)
Nancy Hopkins + Brent Kennedy
(1929–)   (1928–)
N. Brent Kennedy
(1950–)

Reeves—Phipps Line

George Reeves, Sr. + Jane Burton
(1705–?)   (?)
Betty Reeves + Samuel Phipps
(1765–1845)   (1762–1854)
Joseph Phipps + Patty White
(1797–1840)   (1806–1858)
John Wesley Swindall (Phipps/Tolliver) + Mary Polly Phipps
(1826–1900)   (1835–1907)
Elvira "Vie" Swindall + King Solomon Hopkins
(1879–1951)   (1878–1952)
William Sylvester "Taylor" Hopkins + Rexie Nash
(1899–1986)   (1906–1933)
Nancy Hopkins + Brent Kennedy
(1929–)   (1928–)
N. Brent Kennedy
(1950–)

Swindall-Tolliver Line

John Weaver + Barbara Keifer
(1722–?) John fought in the Revolutionary War.
John Swindle + Hannah Weaver
(1746–1839)   (1753–?)
m. 1775, Culpeper VA
John Swindall + Betsy Tolliver
(1778–1853)   (?)
? Phipps + Elizabeth Swindall
(?)   (?)
John Wesley Swindall (Phipps / Tolliver) + Mary Polly Phipps
(1826–1900)   (1835–1907)
Elvira "Vie" Swindall + King Solomon Hopkins
(1879–1951)   (1878–1952)
William Sylvester "Taylor" Hopkins + Rexie Nash
(1899–1986)   (1906–1933)
Nancy Hopkins + Brent Kennedy
(1929–)   (1928–)
N. Brent Kennedy
(1950–)

The Hopkins were a handsome people—although I am
greatly biased. My Grandfather Hopkin's youngest sister Helena
resides in nearby Roswell, Georgia, and we have occasion to get
together even in this busy world. She is a beautiful woman and,
as with my other aunts and uncles, when I look at her and when
we laugh together, I find it incomprehensible that—had the
world not changed—her life's value would have been drastically
lessened. Her dark beauty is uncommon and her heart is big. So
is her tendency toward celebrating life. I will never forget her
going into a little dance in the parking lot of a respected Atlanta
restaurant. Her brother Taylor also had a big heart and early on
successfully set its sights on my grandmother Rexie Nash. Their
marriage produced four daughters, two of whom died of childhood diseases and one who strangled to death on her umbilical

cord. The fourth, Nancy Carroll Hopkins, beat the odds and survived, later giving birth to my brother Richard and to me.

Taylor and Rexie

Rexie and Taylor had many material things, perhaps not from a uptown perspective but certainly from a Melungeon point of view. But Taylor, for all his good traits and basic loving nature, had three faults that when combined would prove catastrophic. First, he had the typical Melungeon chip on the shoulder; second, he drank too much; and third, when he did drink, his anger boiled over onto those who were nearest him. Centuries of pent-up frustration seemed to erupt from this entire generation of Melungeon men. Taylor, like the Nash boys, participated regularly in such emotional purging. But one afternoon it went too far and the history of our family was changed forever.

Taylor and Rexie were both avid hunters, she often accompanying him on his forest trampings, and reportedly a fair markswoman herself. These were apparently fun pastimes, with lots of laughing and teasing and nearly always adding something of substance to the dinner table. One afternoon in mid-October 1933, as Rexie and her sister Edith sat peeling potatoes for the evening's meal, Taylor came in drunk, got out his rifle, and told Rexie—as he had so many times before—that he was going to shoot her. Accustomed to the ritual, she smiled it off and softly told her husband to put the gun away, all the while continuing to peel her potatoes. A moment's hesitation, an ear-splitting explosion, and a panicked Taylor bolted out the door. Rexie died in Edith's arms as two-year old Anna Ruth, only a short time away from dying herself (of colitis), slept in the next room.

Taylor Hopkins (l), administrator Brown Pickle (r),
outside the asylum, two years after Rexie died.

Taylor later claimed it was an accident, that he was drunk, and that he had run not to escape but instead to find help. For a short while Edith supported this version, but later changed her mind. Even today we do not know the truth of what actually happened. But it doesn't matter. Accident or no accident, drunk or sober, he had shot and killed his wife after announcing his intention to do just that. And for that there's no excuse or consolation.

Today, the only living witness, my mother, didn't actually see it occur and probably was too young to understand the events even if she had. In any event, Taylor didn't get far before Rexie's brothers, Bo and Bob, received the terrible news, grabbed their pistols, and went searching for him. Drunk as he was, Taylor somehow escaped their eyes, hiding out in the mountains for three days before turning himself in to the authorities. He had climbed a tall tree and hid among the branches, watching Bob and Bo, breathing fire and cursing his name, tramp to and fro on the forest floor below. And he waited until nightfall before coming down and making his way to the authorities.

A quick trial, a declaration of insanity, and three years in the state asylum in Marion, Virginia were Taylor's compensation for that black and lightning-quick deed in the kitchen of his home. His two surviving girls were taken in by Granny Nash and the already tired matriarch did her best to rear them. What difference would two more

Nancy Hopkins, with her father (face ripped off photo).

mouths make in an already stretched-thin household? But there was no end to the sorrow. Anna Ruth died in 1935, and Momma can still remember Granny and her aunts wailing to the heavens, wringing their hands in a never-ending display of anguish. Three years later, when Momma was nine, she would experience the same scenario upon Bo's murder. It was a way of life on Coeburn Mountain. Untimely death, lonely crushing sorrow, and loss. Always loss.

Poignantly and just as painfully, after her father's release from the asylum, Momma would become accustomed to his ritualized arrival at the Nash homestead. Taylor would stand at the gate at the end of the yard, knowing not to step foot on Nash property, and someone would ferry his daughter out, exchanging the minimum number of words necessary to conduct the business at hand. He would take her for the day, buy her anything she wanted, show her off to his family who would prepare lavish meals in her honor. And out in the yard, he would take her hands and swing her 'round and 'round his spinning body, Momma laughing and begging him to stop as he called her his "little Black Nash." And then sometimes, when alone, he would try to tell her that it had all been an accident, that he never meant to hurt Rexie. Then he'd he take her home.

Once back on the mountain there was the traditional scrub-down as Granny would symbolically—and literally—wash away any dirt, or sins, that she might have picked up through association with her murdering father and his family. It was hard on Momma, enjoying herself immensely, but always having to endure the inevitable washing away of the time spent with her father, as if those hours were somehow evil. But just as a washing would fail to remove the melanin from Momma's skin, neither could it remove the memory of being with one's parent. Regardless of what he had done, he was still her daddy, and symbolically exorcising him did far more harm than good. And yet, in Granny's defense the mere fact that she permitted Momma to spend any time at all with Grandpa bespeaks a forgiveness of sorts. Somehow Granny knew that Momma and Taylor still needed one another, and Granny set her anguish aside often enough to let nature take at least something of its course.

It is a painful memory, but when I was a little boy Grandpa Hopkins would try to do the same with me. He did not come by my father's service station all that often, but when he did he would hug me, look at me pitifully with those strangely light blue eyes—the same ones he handed down to me—and tell me that it had all been a terrible, terrible accident. That he had loved Rexie with all his heart and would never have harmed her. And, all of ten years old, I would tell him I knew that to be the case. Then he would give me a couple dozen of the biggest, shiniest apples his trees had produced, climb back into his antiquated farm truck, and, as tears welled in his eyes, wave goodbye and drive off. And I would go home and write him a letter which he would always answer. Today I realize what agony he was experiencing: a life of ultimate loss, guilt, and regret. And always on the outside of what might have been. At his death in 1986, I said a special prayer that somehow he and Rexie could now patch things up and finish out the great unfinished business of loving each other.

Momma

Even though her last name was Hopkins, Momma grew up as a Nash. Her aunts served as her sisters: Eulalia Oatie, or "Buddie" as she preferred to be called, my godmother Helen, and Edith, Ethel, Thelma, Ruble, Ada, and Trula—all dark beauties and all mother hens to little Nancy. Buddie and Helen, perhaps more than the others, would serve as surrogate mothers to Momma, with Helen particularly doting on my brother and me. Of course, Aunt Helen still lived on Coeburn Mountain, a mere five miles from our home in town, and was more accessible than the others who had moved away. Knowing them, if they'd lived in Wise they'd all undoubtedly done a lot of doting. That was just their way—closing ranks to take care of family.

Most of the Nash girls had gone to Akron, Ohio at the outbreak of World War II, securing jobs in the Goodrich and Goodyear rubber companies. When the war ended, Buddie, Ada, Thelma, and Edith stayed in Ohio, enjoying their new lives as "northerners." Helen came home, maybe because of the abuse she took from coworkers on the assembly line who delighted in calling her "the black Italian." Aunt Helen married Kentuckian Holmes Mayo, one of God's wonderful creations, and they produced my cousin Jennifer. "Jenni," along with Steven Moore and Teresa Stevens, were the three closest "cousin-friends" I had growing up. Steven's mother was Momma's first cousin Shirley Skeen, while his father was Vernoy Moore, himself a descendant of old Eth Moore, a shrewd businessman and a well-known Melungeon, and, on his mother's side, the Sextons of Stone Mountain. Teresa was the daughter of my uncle Bert Stevens and his wife, my aunt Ruble Nash Stevens. Teresa, Steven, and Jennie were all good-looking, dark-haired, dark-eyed Melungeon children, and together we explored a high percentage of the magical forest haunts of Coeburn Mountain, Virginia. But we grew up, and some of us had to leave the area to make our living.

Momma also grew up, and left the mountain on a daily basis to go to Wise High School. There her good looks, intelligence, and outgoing personality made her popular with most everybody.

This is not to say that her background and her dark complexion did not haunt her; it did. How does one selectively forget the shame of being Melungeon? Of a well-meaning but long-suffering grandmother who bundled you up so miserably during the scorching summer months? Granny loved "Little Nancy" and was doing all in her power to prevent another child of the family from reliving her own painful nightmare. Better to look "crazy like a Melungeon" and sweat buckets in mid-July than to darken and pay the price of ostracism. But what a difficult chore to hide from the sun, especially for a little girl who only wanted to play. And then to have Granny's worst fears confirmed by the cruelty of outsiders. To be called "Black Nash" by insensitive townsfolk. To be accused by a college teacher of having not properly washed—and sent back to the showers in front of your classmates—when your own cleanliness exceeded that of your tormentor's. And to take that second bath, knowing full well that nothing would change. To have your neck scrubbed to the point of bleeding in an attempt to remove unremovable melanin.

These are the legacies of being Melungeon, or any "person of color" for that matter. And the little girl or boy that must endure these indignities cannot move through life, at least in this nation, as effortlessly as children with paler complexions. There is a toll taken, a price extracted. Even in later years, such abuse leaves its scars. Ask my mother, or any other American whose physical countenance does not fit the accepted Anglo standards.

But aside from the occasional callous remark and the prejudice of a few ignorant townsfolk, Mother's school life in Wise was more than tolerable. She had many friends, including others who shared her heritage. The principal of the school, L. F. Addington, helped her with her confidence early on. Seeing Momma sit at her desk with her arms turned awkwardly upward, Luther Addington took her aside and asked why she would position herself so uncomfortably. He coaxed from her the intended strategy to appear "whiter" by concealing her darker outer arms, and then L. F. Addington said something to my mother that no outsider ever had: "Why Nancy, you're a pretty girl," he said. "You have a beautiful complexion. Be proud of it!"

It was one of those defining moments in her life. She went on to become an active participant in many school activities, was a straight-A student, and was voted "Best All Around" her senior year. Oh, what dark-skinned people can do when given even the simplest encouragement. I weep for all those who did not, and still do not, have an L. F. Addington to take notice of their plight. To serve up a tiny sliver of humanity in a world bent on beating people down. Whatever L. F. Addington may or may not have done in his life, I am convinced that that one simple little kindness earned him a special place in heaven. To this day, Momma credits Mr. Addington with giving her back a small piece of her dignity.

Chapter 4

No Place to Hide
Part 2. Daddy's Side

Back in the mid-1940s, Brent Kennedy's family lived in one of the finest homes in Wise, Virginia. It must have seemed a world away from Granny's little frame house on Coeburn Mountain. While Granny's place was clean as a whistle, it lacked indoor plumbing and electricity. Brent Kennedy's house, on the other hand, had it all: electricity, indoor plumbing, radiator heat, three or four cars always sitting on the wide, concrete driveway, and a view of the whole town a quarter mile below. These were rich people, at least in 1946. But they were not typical rich folks, for the Melungeon legacy had left its scars on the Kennedys as well.

Brent's daddy Napoleon Bonapart Kennedy—"N. B." to most folks—was himself half Melungeon. A short, powerfully built man with black hair, dark brown eyes, and an olive complexion, he had been on his own since he was eleven, having had a terrible falling out with his stepmother. He survived, however, by hauling water for lumberjacks over Caney Ridge, his homeplace, in Dickenson County. He would sleep in their cabins or tents, or wherever he might find shelter. For a while in his teens he did motorcycle stunts and other unsavory tasks for county fairs to earn his meals. If he was ever afraid of anything, he hid it well. And somewhere during what must have been a hard, uncompro-

mising, and very lonely childhood—if one can call it a childhood—he promised himself that someday he would have a life.
And he did, sort of.

By hook or crook, N. B. Kennedy amassed what was a fortune for his time. A sixteen-room mansion with a small ballroom
and a twenty-five-foot-long dining room overlooking Wise, a 400-
acre Scott County, Virginia farm with two stables and forty race
horses, several dozen rental homes, three restaurants, an auto-
mobile dealership, and on and on. All from nothing. People were
afraid of him, and probably with good reason. He once paid a
fine—in advance—for beating up a man who had offended him.
He had henchmen, hired thugs, who would look after his inter-
ests and he despised anyone that he felt looked down on him.

He ran liquor in Chicago in the 1920s and 1930s, and he
later learned the gaming and pinball business in New Orleans,
supposedly under Carlos Marcello—accused in several best-sell-
ing books of masterminding the assassination of John Fitzgerald
Kennedy. It is doubtful Granddaddy knew Marcello personally,
if he knew him at all; he was more likely a simple hired hand
who kept quiet and learned the mechanics of the business before
taking his newfound knowledge home. And he did take it home.
The result was Kennedy Amusement Company, a thriving enter-
tainment business in the mountains of Virginia, West Virginia,
and Kentucky that flourished until the early 1960s. As a child
I accompanied my father on his assigned rounds to all the little
mountain honky-tonks as he collected bag after bag of change
from what seemed like a million flashing pinball machines. We
would count the change on faux red-marble tabletops, giving the
proprietor his cut before moving on to the next "joint."

My grandfather was a complex man. Despite a toughness
that sometimes bordered on cruelty, he would spy some poor
child on the street, take him or her by the hand and walk into
the nearest department store. There he would outfit the child
with a new suit of clothes, the best shoes, and whatever else
struck his fancy. Then he would buy the child a meal, perhaps
an ice cream cone, and give him some spending money. He cared
for these children, undoubtedly doing for them what he secretly
wished someone had done for him. And when we would have

meals at Granddaddy's house, he would always make sure no one left the table hungry, literally pushing spoonfuls of food into mouths just opening to say, "No more, thank you." And we would dine on such delicacies as strong leeks, buttermilk, fried poke, pork chops, and tomato gravy—far tastier than it may sound, with the gravy, as I have since learned, a subtle hint at our origins.

I remember Granddaddy reminiscing on his favorite book, *Black Beauty*, and how his eyes would brighten when he told of the mistreated horse who broke away from its cruel master and rose to greatness. That was Granddaddy, the mistreated child who broke his bonds and raced his heart out to the finish line. It is probably why he always loved horses; I know he never mistreated one. But life took its toll, and one afternoon as he walked across main street in Norton, Virginia, he collapsed. Nine years later, unable to move or speak from the day of his stroke, he died.

Hornes, Osbornes, Alleys, Powers, and Adkins

Grandaddy was descended from David Kennedy, who along with four brothers—John Fletcher, James, William, and Samuel—supposedly migrated from Northern Ireland sometime around 1760. David (1746–1800) was a lieutenant colonel in the "Cherokee Expedition" of the French and Indian Wars, and served under Captain Peter Hull at Yorktown. He married Mary Elizabeth Conway in 1794, and it was their son, John Fletcher Kennedy, who married a Melungeon girl, Mary Horne.

Mary was the daughter of Pleasant Horne (1781–1865) and Hulda Osborne (1788–1863), both of North Carolina. Pleasant Horne's father, Jesse Horne, was supposedly Scotch-Irish and born in North Carolina in 1777, which would have made him fourteen years of age at the birth of his son. This could be factual, but it is more likely another example of fabricated roots. Hulda was supposedly the daughter of Solomon Osborne and Hannah Bowling and a sister to Sherwood Osborne, the same family line on my Mother's side.

Kennedy Line

Jesse Horne + Nancy Langley
(1777–?)   (?)
Pleasant Horne + Hulda Osborne
(1781–1865)   (1788–1863)
Mary Horne + John Fletcher Kennedy
(1806–?)   (1797–1888)
Pleasant H. Kennedy + Rachel Jane Powers
(1831–1916)   (1828–1881)
Forrest T. Kennedy + Sarah Jane Adkins
(1849–1926)   (1851–1932)
David Kennedy + Ida Powers
(1880–1959)   (1884–1903)
Napoleon B. Kennedy + Tessie Colley
(1903–1986)   (1899–1988)
N. Brent Kennedy + Nancy Hopkins
(1928–   )   (1929–   )
N. Brent Kennedy
(1950–   )

*Rev. Forrest T. Kennedy
and Sarah Jane Adkins*

John Fletcher Kennedy and Mary Horne had ten children, one of whom was Pleasant H. Kennedy (1831–1916), a Union sympathizer who, along with his brother Solomon Kennedy, was jailed by Confederates in Abingdon, Virginia in 1862. Pleasant escaped by leaping from his second-story cell, which was a "pleasant" happenstance for those of us who are descended from him, but Sol was taken from the jail and, some distance from the town, executed by pistol.

Winfield Kennedy   *Rachel Jane Powers Kennedy*

Pleasant's wife was Rachel Jane Powers (1828–1881), the daughter of Forest Powers and Mary "Polly" Alley (1797–?) of Russell County, Virginia. Mary Polly was probably Melungeon, the granddaughter of James Alley, Sr. and his "Black Dutch" wife, Christiana, last name unknown.

Mary Polly's father Joseph Alley, Sr. had also married a Melungeon woman, Mary, last name unknown but thought to be a Collins, from Scott County, Virginia. One of Mary Polly's brothers, Thomas Alley (1788–1864) married Amelia Hubbard of Ashe County, North Carolina, supposedly one-half Cherokee. While this is entirely possible, Ashe County was a heavy Melungeon—as opposed to Cherokee—population center, with most, if not all, true Cherokees, residing farther south. Regardless, Rachel Jane Powers brought to her union with Pleasant Kennedy what must have been the substantial Melungeon heritage of Forest Powers and Mary Polly Alley.

Pleasant Kennedy got religion in a serious way shortly after his narrow escape from execution. He spawned a horde of well-known Presbyterian and Primitive Baptist, Bible-thumping, horseback evangelists, including two preacher sons, John G. Kennedy and Forrest T. Kennedy.

Forrest T. Kennedy was the father of another Appalachian minister, local icon John G. Kennedy, as well as my great-grandfather David Fletcher Kennedy (1880–1959), an eloquent, self-educated Wise, Virginia barrister.

Adkins-Bowman Line

Henry Adkins + Sally Bowman
(1700s, North Carolina)
John Adkins + ?
(?) (?)
Dave Garland + Hannah Adkins
(?) (?)
Sarah Jane Adkins + Forrest T. Kennedy
(1851–1932) (1849–1926)
David Kennedy + Ida Powers
(1880–1959) (1884–1903)
Napoleon B. Kennedy + Tessie Colley
(1903–1986) (1899–1988)
N. Brent Kennedy + Nancy Hopkins
(1928–) (1929–)
N. Brent Kennedy
(1950–)

Forrest T. Kennedy married a North Carolina Melungeon named Sarah Jane Adkins (1851–1932). Sarah Jane was the granddaughter of Henry Adkins and Sally Bowman, both from Ashe County, North Carolina. Sarah Jane's mother, Hannah Adkins, had been abandoned by Sarah Jane's father, a Virginian named Dave S. Garland, and she was raised by her grandparents who placed their surname on her in lieu of Dave's, thus keeping her an Adkins. Dave apparently returned to his Virginia homesite, possibly Amherst County, Virginia. A David S. Garland was indeed alive and well in Amherst County in 1854, and was listed as a "free person of color" along with the other so-called "Buffalo Ridge Cherokees," the previously mentioned "mixed-race" Indian population residing in Amherst County and nearby areas of central Virginia.[1] It is possible that this David S., or possibly a son by the same name, was the father of Sarah Jane Adkins.

John G. Kennedy, Sally Horn Kennedy, and children, ca. 1900.
(John G. was a son of Forrest T. Kennedy.)

Unlike some of Forrest T.'s and Sarah Janes's other children, my great-grandfather David Fletcher did not look all that "Melungeon," and I can still vividly remember his occasional visits to our home in the late 1950s. He was a short, dapper gentleman, with just a hint of swarthiness, who would always pat me on the head and tell me what a fine young man I was. Momma would fix him lunch which he would eat as he chatted away, and then he would wipe his mouth with his handkerchief,

---

[1]Sherrie S. McLeRoy and Wiliam R. McLeRoy, *Strangers in Their Midst: The Free Black Population of Amherst County, Virginia* (Bowie MD: Heritage Books, 1993). [Address: Heritage Books, 1540-E Pointer Ridge Place, Bowie MD 20716.]

thank us, excuse himself, and return to the County Courthouse less than a mile away.

David Kennedy, Parkas Dewitt Kennedy, Ida Powers Kennedy, and N. B. Kennedy, ca. 1903.

Knowing David Fletcher Kennedy, it is hard to understand how he and my grandfather N. B. Kennedy ever fell out. But fall out they did, which is why Granddaddy ran away. Actually, Granddaddy fell out with his stepmother Nannie, who he asserted until his dying day had mistreated him. It is hard to know for sure, since Granddaddy was a highly spirited, and most probably a highly undisciplined, child, but he did leave and Great-grandfather David Fletcher sided with his second wife. Still, to let an eleven-year-old child, rebellious or not, go out on its own is pretty hard to fathom. By the time "D. F.," as they called him, was visiting with us, he and Granddaddy had long since patched things up, at least on the surface. This truce, however, never extended to Nannie and, as far as I know, my grandfather had little or nothing to do with her in his adult years.

David Fletcher Kennedy's first wife Ida M. Powers (1884–1903) died in childbirth, a mere year after bringing my tenacious grandfather into the world. Ida was only nineteen years old at her death, and yet her lone surviving photograph, the top of the head torn off by some careless family member, shows the tired, battered face of a much older woman. Her life must have been hard, as well as unfairly brief. To lose your first child, give birth to a second, live in squalid poverty, and then die while birthing your third baby—all before your twentieth birthday—seems wretchedly harsh. Surely there is a special place in heaven for people like Ida Powers. A place where she can finish her life before joining the saints.

Ida Power's father Winfield Scott Powers, partly Melungeon himself, had married Lucinda Mullins, the daughter of first cousins Andrew "Brandy Jack" Mullins and Polly Anna Mullins (for genealogy, see the "Mullins-Stanley Line" in previous chapter). In the process my brother and I received yet another shot of Old Booker Mullins' genes. A few more such injections and we could easily have been an incarnation of old Booker himself. If that is not enough, through this same marriage we also got yet another dose of the genes of "Spotted Dave" Mullins and Jane Short (parents of Polly Anna), as well as, respectively, their brother and sister "Sherd" Mullins and his wife Anne Short (parents of Brandy Jack). I can visualize all this recombinant DNA joining together at each such union, much like surprised relatives bumping into each other at a TupperWare party, "My goodness, what are you doing here?" So much for genetic diversity. But then, to beg the question, what choice did we have?

The Name Game

Beyond the DNA question, it is hard to keep track of one's paper genealogy when one is a Melungeon. This is primarily because more than half of southwest Virginia's Melungeon families were Mullinses, and each family seemed to have some sort of a secret pact to give their children the same names. I have found five Andrew Jackson Mullinses living at the same time! Some mysteries of family connections will undoubtedly never be solved, since it is next to impossible to distinguish between, as yet another example, eight "John Mullinses" residing practically in the same hollow a century and a half ago. Only when something unusual happens to one of them, such as "Brandy Jack" going to jail for counterfeiting, can we speak with confidence about which one was which. This may be part of the reason we Melungeons have lost our sense of identity: we all have the same name!

Nevertheless, some of us have tried to bring a semblance of order to the process of ferreting out our ancestry. In 1941, David Fletcher Kennedy's brother W. P. Kennedy, wrote a little history of the family entitled *The Name and Family of Kennedy and Powers*. It is a good piece of work with much useful information and invaluable photographs of Sarah Jane Adkins Kennedy and Rachel Jane Powers Kennedy. When viewing the photographs of these two striking if somewhat intimidating ladies, there is no doubt that, contrary to the book's assertions, they were not full Scotch-Irish. In both women, their raven-black hair, dark complexions, high cheekbones, and dark eyes leap out at the viewer. I am a bit surprised that W. P. included these telltale photos, since he obviously—and purposefully—excluded any reference to Brandy Jack, Sherd, and Booker Mullins, as well as Anne and Jane Short. While he may have felt it safe to talk about earlier, unrecognizable Melungeon ancestors, those other Mullinses and Shorts were too close for comfort and certainly well known as Melungeons. Consequently, they did not even earn a footnote in W. P.'s book. Given the times, we can scarcely blame him, and even today there will certainly be those family members who will applaud this exclusion. But the present text is my history, those Melungeons are part of me, and I am proud of them and I want them in it.

Colleys, Counts, Kisers, and Kennedys

In 1918, N. B. Kennedy married a schoolteacher/mountain midwife five years his senior, Tessie Colley (1899–1988). Since Granddaddy was but fifteen when he married the twenty-year old Tessie, it is possible he was in part looking for a combination wife and mother. It is also possible that, having been on his own for four years, he just needed a little more security in his life. Tessie undoubtedly represented that security. N. B. and Tessie's marriage ended, after twelve years, on a rather sour note, my grandfather not being the settling-down type and not particularly forgiving after being crossed. We have no evidence that Tessie crossed him, except for standing up to him, but it was probably a marriage that should never have been. Of course, I am most grateful for its occurrence so that I could be here to write reasons as to why it should never have been.

The union produced six children: four girls and two boys. One of the boys was my father Brent Kennedy. The other boy, Kenneth, died at the age of twenty-four in a 1947 coal-mining accident. It was a terrible incident that left its mark indelibly ripped into my grandfather's psyche.

One afternoon when Kenneth didn't return home as expected, my grandfather went looking for him at the private, isolated coal mine where he worked. It was a two-man operation, Kenneth's first business venture on his own, and his last. Granddaddy found his body a few feet from the entrance of the mine, his stiffened fingers frozen around the collar of a dead coworker he had tried to rescue. Both had succumbed to the invisible deadliness of carbon monoxide fumes escaping from a faulty generator. My grandfather scooped up his son's body and ran in a blind panic toward his truck. In his grief he became confused and inexplicably ran into the forest where rescuers would later discover him—collapsed on his knees, staring straight ahead, the lifeless body of his son lying across his lap. The men had to forcibly pry his fingers apart to retrieve Kenneth's body. Emotionally, he never did let go.

Some fifteen years later, when I was twelve years old, I would watch from the shadows as my father broke the news of yet another mining death. A young miner had been electrocuted in an accident and several men had come by our service station to ask dad to tell Claude, the young man's father, of his son's death. There was no telephone at the mine where Claude worked, and it was the old man's custom to stop by my dad's station following each evening's shift for "nabs and a dope," that is, crackers and a Pepsi. Dad was upset, but agreed to tell Claude that his only son had been killed. When Claude's old truck pulled up out front, I hid behind the parts counter, my heart pounding a thousand beats a minute. As my dad did what he had to do, as gently as he knew how, Claude dropped his nabs, moaned, and crumpled in on himself. I watched as my dad, who by nature struggled with showing his emotions, slowly embraced a devastated old man, and sobbed along with him.

Granddaddy had earlier used his considerable money and influence, already keen at the age of twenty-seven, to win custody of the children from Tessie. N. B.'s father, D. F., apparently also intervened to keep the grandchilden in Wise, and Tessie, having little legal or financial resources, never had a chance to counter. Beaten badly by a stacked legal system, she had no choice but to move as far away from Wise County as she possibly could. Forcibly denied contact with her children, she finally surrendered all hope of reestablishing those relationships. It was not until my early twenties, some forty-five years later, that I discovered I had a grandmother living somewhere in Florida, tracked her down, and discovered an intellectually vibrant but physically crippled old woman who had lost all hope of reconnecting. But we did reconnect, and shared much laughter and a few tears over a life that might have been. And from her I learned more than I can ever express: philosophies of life and love, a keener understanding of family, an expanded sense of the spiritual and the divine, and a factual roadmap of her own lineage.

Tessie was descended from Thomas Colley (1720–1800), a captain in the Battle of King's Mountain. Along with his wife Judith, Thomas had come to Reeds Valley in Russell County, Virginia shortly before his death in 1783, making them possibly the first permanent settlers of what is now Dickenson County, Virginia. We do not know the nationality of Judith, although it is possible she was either Melungeon or part Indian. It may also be relevant that we likewise do not know with any surety the origins of Thomas Colley himself. In any event, Thomas and Judith produced nine children, one of whom was the famous frontiersman Richard "Fighting Dick" Colley. "Fighting Dick" was quite a man and tough as nails: they say he beat an attacking bear to death with his fists in front of witnesses. This is not to say he was not shredded up pretty badly by the bear in return, but he survived and the bear did not. And so a legend was born.

Colley-Counts Line

Thomas Colley + Judith ?
(?)   (?)
Richard "Fighting Dick" Colley + Christina (*) Counts
*(variously "Lucretia" or "Crissa")
(1783–1858)   (1793–1855)
John Colley + Annie Davis
(?)   (?)
Jasper S. Colley + "Peg" Sutherland
(?)   (1845–1944)
m. Nov. 1866
Major Pelham Colley + Hester Kiser
(1873–?)   (1879–?)
Tessie Colley + Napoleon B. Kennedy
(1899–1988)   (1903–1986)
Brent Kennedy + Nancy Hopkins
(1928–   )   (1929–   )
Brent Kennedy
(1950–   )

Fighting Dick married Lucretia "Crissa" Counts, supposedly a descendant of a 1730s German immigrant named Joseph Kuntz, although there is no proof of this connection. Joseph's son John Counts (?–1803) married Mary Magdaline (?–1814) in Russell County, Virginia. We know little of Mary Magdaline, either, except there is some mention—but no evidence—that she may have been "Cherokee." And for some reason, John Counts later passed himself off as "Black Dutch," that is, those Dutch descended from the sixteenth-century Spanish and Portuguese who occupied Holland. Perhaps his mother, Joseph Kuntz's unnamed wife, was Melungeon or Indian, and this was John's attempt to explain his darker features. Or maybe they truly were "Black Dutch." At this late date, we just do not know and probably never will.

What we do know, however, is that Fighting Dick's and Crissa's children—John Counts's grandchildren—married into various Melungeon families: two children married Mullinses and one, my great-great-great-uncle James Colley (1815—1887), married Emma Farrell (1815–1885). Emma's mother was Jane Jackson, one of the "Black Jacksons" of western North Carolina (although Jane would always disclaim any relationship). Their sibling, my great-great-grandfather Jasper S. Colley, married "Peg" Sutherland, the daughter of James Sutherland and Nancy Counts. Jasper's father John Colley, a son of "Fighting Dick," married Annie Davis, daughter of Jefferson Davis of Grayson County, Virginia. "Davis" is a common Melungeon surname and Grayson County—snuggled up next to the North Carolina border—lay in the heart of seventeenth-century Melungeon territory. "Davis" was also a quite common last name among the Buffalo Ridge Cherokees of central Virginia. Jasper S. Colley and Peg Sutherland produced Major Pelham Colley, a dark-haired, black-eyed, brooding man who married Hester Kiser, also a descendant of John and Mary Magdaline Counts. Major Pelham Colley and Hester Kiser were my Grandmother Tessie's parents.

Counts-Jesse Line

John Counts + Mary Magdelene (?)
(?)   (?)
John Counts + Margaret Kelly
(?)   (?)
Jefferson Jessee + Nancy Counts
(1802–1861)   (1803–1880)
Reverend Abednigo Kiser + Margaret Jessee
(1833–1915)   (1838–1902)
Major Pelham Colley + Hester Kiser
(1873–?)   (1879–?)
Tessie Colley + Napoleon Kennedy
(1899–1988)   (1903–1986)
Brent Kennedy + Nancy Hopkins
(1928–   )   (1929–   )
N. Brent Kennedy
(1950–   )

Hester's German ancestry went back to Carl Kayser who had migated from Württemberg, Germany in 1749, later serving in Braddock's army in 1755. Hester's great-grandfather Joseph Kiser had brought his wife Susannah Stacey to Russell County, Virginia where Hester's grandfather, the Reverend Elihugh Kiser (1810–?), was born. Elihugh in turn married Virginia "Jane" Skeen (1811–?) and, among other children, they gave us Hester's father, the Reverend Abednigo Kiser (1832–1917).

It is possible that Joseph Kiser's wife Susannah Stacey was of Melungeon descent, and it is almost a certainty that Abednigo's wife Margaret Jessee, the daughter of Jefferson Jessee and Nancy Counts (yes, the same Counts line again), was partly Melungeon. The North Carolina roots of Jefferson Jessee's family, as well as the Jessee name being an associated Melungeon surname, provide tantalizing circumstantial evidence that Margaret was indeed Melungeon.

Regardless of how these darker genes may have slipped in, by the early 1800s both the Kisers and the Colleys were a dark-complexioned, black and curly-haired people alternately claiming an Indian or "Black Dutch" heritage.

Elihugh Kiser and Jane Skeen Kiser, ca. 1860.

Kiser Line

Carl (Charles) Kayser + ? Shelley
(from Germany, 1749)
Joseph Kiser + Susannah Stacey
(?–1816)   (?)
Abednigo Kiser + Mary Polly Jessee
(1784–1814)   (?)
Rev. Elihugh Kiser + Virginia "Jane" Skeen
(1810–?)   (1811–?)
Rev. Abednigo Kiser + Margaret Jessee
(1833–1915)   (1838–1902)
Major Pelham Colley + Hester Kiser
(1873–?)   (1879–?)
Tessie Colley + Napoleon Kennedy
(1899–1988)   (1903–1986)
Brent Kennedy + Nancy Hopkins
(1928–   )   (1929–   )
N. Brent Kennedy
(1950–   )

Davis-Colley-Sutherland Line

Jefferson Davis + (?)
(Grayson County, Virginia)
Annie Davis + John Colley
(?)   (?)
Jasper S. Colley + Margaret "Peg" Sutherland
(m. Nov. 1866)   (1845–1944)
Major Pelham Colley + Hester Kiser
(1873–?)   (1879–?)
Tessie Colley + Napoleon Kennedy
(1899–1988) (1903–1986)
Brent Kennedy + Nancy Hopkins
(1928–   ) (1929–   )
N. Brent Kennedy
(1950–   )

Hester Kiser and Major Pelham Colley had four children, Tessie, Bernice, Elsie, and Elmer. We know now Tessie married N. B. Kennedy and among their six children—each of whom was at least one-third Melungeon if not more—was my father, Napoleon Brent Kennedy. And with Brent Kennedy's marriage to Nancy Hopkins, at least thirteen, and possibly as many as sixteen, so-called "Melungeon branches" came together in my brother and me.

Hester Kiser Colley, age 16, 1895.

Major Pelham and Hester Colley, with Tessie (l) and Elsie (r), ca. 1902.

Chapter 5

Genesis: Whence We Came

So who are we? As I quickly discovered after leaping into the quandary of trying to answer this question, there were varying theories regarding the origins of the Melungeon people, ranging from serious anthropologically based efforts to fantasy-inspired supposition. The most popular theories are as follows.

1. *Surviving descendants of the "Lost Colony" of Roanoke Island who later intermarried with Native Americans.* The "Elizabethan English" spoken by the first-encountered Melungeons, as well as their English surnames, have been cited as evidence in support of this theory. Many past researchers have argued that, given English surnames and use of the English language, albeit broken English, the Melungeons must be of English origin. However, the "Mediterranean appearance" of so many Melungeons, as well as their original denial of either an English or Indian heritage argue against a purely Lost Colony and/or English hypothesis.

These same researchers likewise conveniently overlook the fact that African-Americans also assumed English surnames and spoke English, but only as survival mechanisms. And while there may well be an English component within the early Melungeon population, the argument for a primary English origin based purely on surnames and nonfluent language usage is, consequently, weak at best.[1]

2. *Descendants of the Welsh explorer "Madoc,"[2] who supposedly trounced around the Southern Appalachians in the 1100s A.D.* There is absolutely nothing to support this theory, except that Madoc may actually have been in the Southern Appalachians. Certainly the Melungeons do not look Welsh.

3. *One of the "lost tribes" of Israel.[3]* It is an interesting theory, but there is very little evidence beyond the discovery of a few second-century Hebrew Bar Kokhba coins in Kentucky, coins that could have been lost by later explorers, Jewish settlers, or even planted as a hoax. And although there may be a Jewish ethnic component within the Melungeon population, there is scant evidence to suggest that this component arrived on these shores thousands of years ago.

4. *Descendants of early Carthaginian, or perhaps Phoenician, seamen who may have discovered the New World some 2,000*

---

[1]A similarly fascinating theory exists regarding a supposed relationship between the Lost Colony survivors and the Lumbees of North Carolina. Tindall notes that "The only clue [of what happened to the Lost Colony] was one word carved on a doorpost, 'Croatoan,' the name of a friendly tribe of Indians and also of their island, the present Ocracoke. A romantic legend later developed that the colonists joined the Croatan Indians, finally were absorbed by them, and were among the ancestors of the present Lumbee Indians of Robeson County, North Carolina." George Brown Tindall, *America. A Narrative History* (New York: W. W. Norton, 1984) 39.

[2]Madog ab Owain Gwynedd, a Welsh prince, fl. 1170, may be legendary, but according to Richard Hakluyt's *Voyages* (1582) and David Powel's *Historia of Cambria* (1584), he sailed away in ten ships and discovered America ca. 1170. His popular name is from Robert Southey's epic poem *Madoc* (1805).

[3]The fall of the Northern Kingdom (Israel) of the Hebrews ca. 722/1 B.C. with the subsequent dispersion of the Israelites has given rise to the popular "lost ten tribes" notion. (Ten and not twelve tribes because Judah and Benjamin to the south were not overrun until ca. 587/6.) Those ten tribes eventually were "lost" by amalgamation, of course, in much the same way the Melungeons have been misplaced.

years before the birth of Christ. The Melungeons' physical characteristics mesh almost perfectly with this theory, and old Melungeon legends even give a boost to a previous North African existence. Even the seventeenth-century French, upon encountering
the Melungeons in east Tennessee, thought them to be not
Indians but "Moors" and Moors are the direct descendants of the
Carthaginians.

However, even if such an ancient Atlantic crossing occurred,
and, it seems highly unlikely that the surviving population could
have maintained—for no less than 3,500 years—a separate existence, both culturally and genetically, from the Native Americans. In that period of time, the Carthaginians would most likely
have been either absorbed totally into, or destroyed by, the already sizable Native American tribes. It would also not explain
their persistent claim to be "Portyghee," in addition to "Moors"
and "Turks."

5. *Shipwrecked Portuguese sailors.* The earliest Melungeons
invariably claimed to be Portuguese, and occasionally shipwrecked Portuguese. But a skin darker than the English per-
ceived the Portuguese should possess, as well as the use of both
English surnames and Elizabethan English language, have his-
torically been cited as evidence against this theory. Futhermore,
it has generally been thought that there was only a minimal
Portuguese presence along our southeastern coast, yet another
factor arguing against a Portuguese heritage. Nevertheless, even
the skeptics have admitted the difficulty in dismissing outright
the possible Portuguese link, primarily due to the early, widespread nature of these claims among even the most widely separated Melungeon settlements, and seeming cultural and
linguistic evidences.

6. *Finally, the theory that the Melungeons are a simple "tri-
racial isolate," in this particular case the progeny of a few eighteenth-century whites, escaped slaves, and Native Americans.*
While there is definitely Native American and African influence
in at least some, if not all, Melungeon populations, it is far more
complex and probably from a much older source than historians
have generally recognized. What this theory blatantly overlooks
is (1) the sizable Melungeon population that existed prior to

1750 and its wide geographic spread, (2) the very few "escaped slaves" that resided in the Appalachians at that time period, and, again, (3) the strikingly Mediterranean appearance (as opposed to purely Indian or African) of the earliest known Melungeons. As we shall see, it also ignores much of what we now know to be the history of the Southeast, a history that, once understood, goes a long way toward explaining who the Melungeons really are.

The Persistent Legacies of Will Allen Dromgoole and W. A. Plecker

Much of the closed-mindedness among historians regarding the Melungeons can be traced directly to the pronouncements of two individuals: the first, a nineteenth-century pulp journalist from Nashville whose lack of training as an anthropologist and general insensitivity to others did not interfere with her anthropological pronouncements; the second, the medical registrar of the state of Virginia whose searing racial prejudices approached the horrific. Will Allen Dromgoole, and her later medical counterpart Dr. W. A. Plecker did not know one another, but together wove a tapestry of intense pain and heartache for the Melungeon people, a tapestry that covers us, and other dark-skinned Americans, even today.

The simplifed "tri-racial isolate" theory, as well as the negative image of Melungeons in general, seems to have really taken hold via the 1891 writings of Dromgoole. To quote from her first article on the Melungeons:

> Their complexion is a reddish-brown, totally unlike the Mulatto. . . . They are not at all like the Tennessee mountaineer, either in appearance or characteristics. The mountaineer, however poor, is clean, cleanliness itself. He is honest (I speak of him as a class), he is generous, trustful, until once betrayed, truthful, brave, and possessing many of the noblest and keenest sensibilities. The Malungeons are filthy, their home is filthy. They are rogues, natural, "born rogues," close, suspicious, inhospitable, untruthful, cowardly, and, to

use their own word, "sneaky." In many things they resemble the negro. They are exceedingly immoral, yet are great shouters and advocates of religion. . . . They are an unforgiving people, although, unlike the sensitive mountaineer, they are slow to detect an insult, and expect to be spit upon. But injury to life or property they never forgive."[4]

I still receive photocopies of her work from scholars and other well-meaning individuals who are certain that I have overlooked her "findings" and the obvious truth as already established by Miss Dromgoole. Dromgoole, whether intentional or not, did great historical and emotional damage to the Melungeon people. This woman, after living with a particularly poverty-stricken Melungeon family for several nights, disparaged their home, customs, morals, foodstyles, manners, and intelligence. She failed miserably to grasp the reasons for such poverty, assuming that such a degrading lifestyle was by choice, not circumstance. She also concluded that all Melungeons were descended from two men in the late 1700s, both Cherokee Indians:

> Somewhere in the eighteenth century, before the year 1797, there appeared in the eastern portion of Tennessee, at that time the territory of North Carolina, two strange-looking men calling themselves "Collins" and "Gibson." They spoke in broken English, a dialect distinct from anything ever heard in that section of the country. They claimed to have come from Virginia and many years after emigrating, themselves told the story of their past.
>
> These two, Vardy Collins and Buck Gibson, were the head and source of the Malungeons in Tennessee. With the cunning of their Cherokee ancestors, they planned and executed a scheme by which they were enabled to "set up for themselves" in the almost unbroken territory of North Carolina.

---

[4]Will Allen Dromgoole, "The Malungeons." *The Arena* 3 (March 1891); also "The Malungeon Tree and Its Four Branches," *The Arena* 3 (June 1891).

Old Buck, as he was called, was disguised by a wash of some dark description, and taken to Virginia by Vardy where he was sold as a slave. He was a magnificent specimen of physical strength, and brought a fine price, a wagon and mules, a lot of goods, and three hundred dollars in money being paid to old Vardy for his "likely nigger." Once out of Richmond, Vardy turned his mules' shoes and struck out for the Wilderness of North Carolina, as previously planned. Buck lost little time ridding hmself of his Negro disguise, swore he was not the man bought of Collins, and followed in the wake of his fellow-thief to the Territory. The proceeds of the sale were divided and each chose his habitation; old Vardy choosing Newman's Ridge, where he was joined by others of his race, and so the Malungeons became a part of the inhabitants of Tennessee.

This story I know to be true. There are reliable parties still living who received it from old Vardy himself, who came here as a young man and lived, as the Malungeons generally live, to a ripe old age.

The names "Collins" and "Gibson" were also stolen from the white settlers in Virginia where the men had lived previous to emigrating to North Carolina.[5]

While elements of her story may well be true (for example, the Virginia-North Carolina origin and/or the adoption of Anglo surnames), most of her conclusions are shortsighted, naive, and certainly racist in nature. Ms. Dromgoole, known disaffectionately by the Melungeon people as "Will Allen Damfool," also posited that "Octoroons" (individuals who were one-eighth Melungeon) could not (like mules) biologically reproduce. Later, recognizing that such a belief, if true, would have long ago removed the Melungeons from the face of the earth, she backed off her statement. But the statement survives and really does do a pretty good job of summing up her contribution to our history. But she was undeniably right about one thing: when it came to her, the

---

[5]Will Allen Dromgoole, "The Malungeon Tree and its Four Branches," *The Arena* 3 (June 1891): 745-46.

Melungeon people were forever after "suspicious, inhospitable, and unforgiving." And no "big city journalist" was ever again accepted into their homes.

Sadly, some of Miss Dromgoole's "research" was apparently referred to (with no mention of her name) as late as 20 August 1942 in a letter from the state of Virginia's registrar of vital statistics, Dr. Walker Ashley ("W. A.") Plecker, to the Tennessee state librarian and archivist, Mrs. John Trotman Moore. In the letter, Plecker was upholding Virginia's antimiscegenation laws which prohibited marriages between Melungeons and "whites." Plecker described—with almost Nazi-like delight—his approach to classifying Virginia's citizens by race. And he shares his irritation with the Melungeons who, in his own words,

> are now causing trouble in Virginia by their claims of Indian descent, with the privilege of intermarrying into the white race . . . we have found . . . that none of our Virginia people now claiming to be Indian are free from negro admixture, and they are, therefore, according to our laws, classified as colored. In that class we include the melungeons of Tennessee. . . . Miss Kelly and I would be greatly pleased to talk with you on this and kindred subjects and to show you the work which Miss Kelly is doing in properly classifying the population of Virginia by racial origin. She is doing work which, so far as I know, has never before been attempted.

In fact, Plecker fought most of his life to reclassify all people into one of two racial categories: "White" (that is, northern European) and "Colored" (that is, those with one-sixteenth or more Black, Indian, Asian, or southern European heritage). Those darker Americans who felt no prejudice toward their African brothers and sisters but simply insisted on being who they were (for example, Cherokee, Arab, Hispanic, and so forth) were particular targets of Plecker's wrath. "Trouble-makers" he called them in his correspondence, as he again and again refused to recognize their diverse heritages. If you were not "White," then you were "Colored." Period. In the letter quoted above, he even went on to say that claiming a Portuguese heritage was equally meaningless, since

It is a historical fact, well known to those who have investigated, that at one time there were many African slaves in Portugal. Today there are no true negroes there but their blood shows in the color and racial characteristics of a large part of the Portuguese population of the present day. That mixture, even if it could be shown, would be far from constituting these people white.

Plecker was particularly eager to legally disenfranchise those who fell into the "Colored" category. While we Melungeons can be proud of any African heritage we may possess, we also have a right to embrace any European, Arabic, Turkish, or Indian ancestry as well. Plecker effectively denied us and other "mixed race" peoples such a basic human right. According to historian Helen C. Rountree,

> Plecker was methodical: he began collecting old county and federal records on the Indians, many of which listed them as "persons of color." But Plecker was a doctor, not a historian: he took no interest in the conditions under which the records had been made about illiterate people or in the changes that had occurred in the meanings of words. To him, "color" in 1830 meant the same thing that "color" did in 1930, and if the term appeared in an old document, the negritude of the person so designated was "proved." Even the admonitions of a "neutral" agent like the U.S. commissioner of Indian Affairs could not change Plecker's mind. . . . He and his colleagues therefore set about compiling a "Racial Integrity File," consisting of surviving county and U.S. census documents and also "testimony" from "respected" local people about other people's ancestry. The contents of the file became "proof" of Negro ancestry for a wide variety of Virginians, including the Powhatan tribes.[6]

---

[6]Helen C. Rountree, *Pocahontas's People: The Powhatan Indians of Virginia Through Four Centuries* (Norman: University of Oklahoma

It is absolutely dumbfounding that this twisted human being was permitted to exercise such brutal and punitive control over the lives of so many innocent people. Yet the Commonwealth of Virginia inexplicably permitted him free rein from 1912 until 1946, allowing him to sow seeds of pain and despair that continue to bear their fetid fruit even today. At Plecker's urging the Virginia legislature in 1924 passed the "Racial Integrity Act," which specified that only those with one-sixteenth or less Indian blood could be considered "White." And because American antebellum census records consistently described those with Indian blood as "free Negroes" or "mulattoes," Plecker forced all Indians to be listed as such. Plecker, as much as anyone, was responsible for the loss of so many of the rich ethnic subcultures that once flourished in the South.

David Smith says that Plecker's intent was "documentary genocide," a form of genocide based on an attempt "to destroy completely a race of people, Native Americans, by legislating and bureaucratizing them out of existence. In each instance the people in question were made to be viewed as an inferior strain of humanity. The fact that some of these people survived psychologically and culturally is a testament to their dignity and courage."[7]

No better example of Plecker's intentions can be found than in a letter he wrote to Lee County, Virginia public schools trustee J. P. Kelly in 1930 (see next page, below). This letter also graphically illustrates why racial or ethnic census classifications—even up through the 1930s—cannot always be taken as accurate. Plecker was obviously attempting to change people's classification through coercion.

Plecker's nightmarish campaign eventually came to an end. In 1943 he arbitrarily mailed out edicts to the state's county clerks in which he listed family surnames that should be

Press, 1990) 222.

   [7]J. David Smith, "Dr. Plecker's Assault on the Monacan Indians: Legal Racism and Documentary Genocide," in *Lynch's Ferry Magazine* (Charlottesville VA, Spring/Summer 1992): 22-25.

changed from "Indian" or "White" to "Negro." Even those who

BUREAU OF VITAL STATISTICS
STATE DEPARTMENT OF HEALTH

RICHMOND

W. A. PLECKER, M. D.,
REGISTRAR OF VITAL STATISTICS

August 5, 1930.

Mr. J. P. Kelly,
Trustee of Schools,
Pennington Gap,
Lee County, Virginia.

Dear Sir:

Our office has had a great deal of trouble in reference to the persistence of a group of people living in that section known as "Melungeons", whose families came from Newman's Ridge, Tennessee. They are evidently of negro origin and are so recognized in Tennessee, but when they have come over into Virginia they have been trying to pass as white. In a few instances we learn that they have married a low type of white people which increases the problem.

We understand that some of these negroes attempted to send their children to the Pennington Gap white school and that they were turned out by the School Board. Will you please give us a statement as to the names of the children that were thus refused admittance into the white schools and the names and addresses of their parents. If possible, we desire the full name of the father and the maiden name of the mother.

As these families originated out of Virginia, our old birth, death, and marriage records covering the period, 1853 through 1896, do not have them listed by color as are those whose families have lived in Virginia for a number of generations. They are demanding of us that we register them as white, which we persistently refuse to do. If we can get a statement that the School Board refused them admittance into the white schools, we can use that as one of the grounds upon which we would refuse to classify them as white. That, of course, is a matter of history and does not involve any individual but the whole School Board, the responsibility thus being divided up, while few individuals who write to us as to their negro characteristics are willing to have their names used or to appear in court should it become necessary. This makes it very difficult for us to secure necessary information to properly classify them in our office. If the School Trustees will co-operate with our office and will refuse them admittance into the white schools and give us information when such refusals are made, we can without great difficulty hold them in their place, but this co-operation is very essential.

I do not know who is the Clerk of the School Board or who would be the proper one to apply to but your name has been given to me.

Yours very truly,

W. A. Plecker

WAP:W   State Registrar.

Plecker's letter to J. P. Kelly.

had been sitting on the fence were at last outraged. This final, brazen act of demigod racism was partly responsible for his demise, but he still hung on for three additional years. When at long last he resigned, he finally admitted the illegality of his actions, but the damage was done and it remains with us even today.[8]

After Dromgoole, Plecker's "findings" are the second most common "evidences" mailed to me. Helen Rountree provides an excellent summation of Plecker's efforts to enforce the Racial Integrity Act, as well as a thorough history of the Powhatan and related Indian tribes of Virginia.[9]

The "Tri-Racial Isolate" Theory and Its Unfortunate Results

The "tri-racial isolate" theory, with its accompanying unintended prejudices, has exerted such a chilling influence on attempts to properly and sensitively study indigenous peoples, as well as other early immigrants, that it merits special discussion. This method of classifying people (whereby researchers have lumped virtually all inexplicable, seemingly genetically isolated populations into a simplifed, singular group) has not only been the easy way out of performing more professional, probing research, but has also contributed in a significant way to the actual demise of many rich, precious, and diverse cultures. Although originally intended as an innocent "catch-all" to explain the seemingly unexplainable, this theory became a convenient "box" into which could be dumped that portion of humanity whose claims offended or otherwise conflicted with the Anglo status quo. By denying the possibility that any eighteenth-century cultures other than "English," "Indian," or "slave," or a combination thereof, could possibly exist in eighteenth-century America is not only unrealistic but imperialistic and racist in every sense of these words. To shove all multiethnic people into

---

[8]McLeRoy and McLeRoy, *Strangers in Their Midst*.
[9]Rountree, *Pocahontas's People*, 219-42.

this generic pigeonhole and assign to them a racial label in which they have no input—which is what the tri-racial isolate theory inadvertently did—is an incredibly hostile action.

"Tri-racial isolate" has somehow come to be seen as a separate and precise racial classification, despite its original intent to simply identify a closed, inbreeding population. Those who are arbitrarily assigned to it have effectively been denied the God-given right to claim their national or specific ethnic heritages. It is a thinly veiled attempt to avoid confronting the reality of a truly diverse American ethnic heritage. Plecker is an example of this theory carried to its most extreme form, but the general population of the South seems to have bought into the theory's presumed infallibility.

Furthermore, those present-day scholars who patronizingly criticize members of these "tri-racial isolates" for, in the words of one, "casting about for an ancestry," do not grasp the long-standing histories of the various peoples involved, histories that have always included well-defined self-concepts and longtime declarations of who they are.

Contrary to the belief of some, it has not been the members of the so-called "tri-racial isolates" who have struggled to determine their identities, but instead the historians and census takers who have insisted on turning the established heritages of others into mysteries. Can the descendants of the Jamestown settlers *irrefutably* prove that their famous forebears were truly English? It would be difficult at best, even though there is no doubt that they were. We might further imagine that the Portuguese had eventually conquered the South, forcing the Jamestown settlers to "Portugize" their names and learn broken sixteen-century Portuguese in order to survive. Would we be studying about Jamestown in our Portuguese-language history books? Of course not, for an English settlement at Jamestown would be the simple fantasy of a disenfranchised people "casting about for an ancestry." Such inequitable circumstances, however cruel, are the natural results of the struggle for territory. But we need to remember that such circumstances—and their end-results—have indeed occurred. To think otherwise is to mock the lives and heritages of those who did not win, but did survive.

We are still paying the price for such chicanery. Just a little digging, for example, would show that the Melungeon claim to be "Portyghee" is not a twentieth-century phenomenon, as one university "historian" patiently tried to explain to me. It has been present from the beginning and the slightest bit of research would show this. And the word "Melungeon" did not "suddenly appear" in the late 1800s, as yet another "expert" insisted: our documents irrefutably show its existence in the late 1700s, and as far west as Arkansas in 1810.

Too many researchers have blindly accepted the unsupported work of others—usually inadequately conducted secondary research—as opposed to examining the evidence for themselves. No one can review the literature and not recognize the absurdity of such statements as those represented above. But how much easier it is to just accept that the designation "free person of color" in an eighteenth-century census always meant "Negro" or "mulatto" than to study the social and political climate of the times, and to glean the truth of a deeper, more complex set of circumstances. How much less troublesome to accept the face-value meaning, as defined by ignorant and prejudiced eighteenth-century census takers, than to wonder how—in an era when tremendous financial value was placed on a slave—there were so many "free colored" running about in the mountains. Indeed, in 1795, *in Tennessee alone*, there were 973 "free persons" other than whites listed in the census.[10] Certainly the Melungeons are "tri-racial," but this term in and of itself tells us absolutely nothing about our origins. It is inconceivable that historians have glossed over such incongruencies and the hints they offer.

To gain a better understanding of the history of and rationale for purposefully inaccurate racial classification in federal censuses, I strongly recommend William R. McLeRoy's and Sherrie S. McLeRoy's historical study *Strangers in Their Midst:*

---

[10]Hale and Merritt, *A History of Tennessee and Tennesseans*, vol. 1 (1913) 184.

The Free Black Population of Amherst County, Virginia, where this unfortunate phenomenon is explored.[11]

To close out this topic, I must admit I find it absolutely amazing—no, stupefying—that this critically important story, a story that can revolutionize our understanding of both the settling and ethnic makeup of our nation, has been routinely and consistently relegated to the backburner of academia.

Setting the Stage

Of course, in the beginning I assumed everything I read was correct, the result of qualified digging and documented research. As I struck out on my search for the origins of the Melungeons, I was prepared to discover that we were, as the experts said, a "simple tri-racial isolate" of relatively recent origin. Frankly, I really did not care who we were; just the knowing was important. I had visions of celebrating my ethnic heritage by, for example, redecorating our house with a "Cherokee Room," a "Zulu Room," and a "Celtic Room." And I began reading everything I could get my hands on. I read both Bonnie Ball's and Jean Patterson Bible's books on the Melungeons many times over, and searched out another five dozen newspaper and magazine stories. And as I searched and read, and simultaneously dug deeper into my own family's roots, something remarkable happened. I came to believe the long-discounted Melungeon claim to be of Portuguese—and even Moorish and Turkish—origin. The "Mediterranean look" of my own family certainly seemed to substantiate it, and I found early autobiographical statements from others—some of whom were born in the eighteenth century—claiming a Portuguese ancestry. Why such a consistent clamor over the years to be Portuguese or Turkish if there was indeed no Portuguese or Turkish ancestry?

---

[11]Sherrie S. McLeRoy and William R. McLeRoy, *Strangers in Their Midst: The Free Black Population of Amherst County, Virginia* (Bowie MD: Heritage Books, 1993). [Address: Heritage Books, 1540-E Pointer Ridge Place, Bowie MD 20716.]

Believing the claim and proving it, however, were two differ-ent matters. I was faced with the daunting and unavoidable re-quirement of solving a three-hundred-year-old mystery in order to know my family's ethnic roots. My first instinct was to surren-der, since better minds than mine had tried and failed. And yet, those cries from the grave kept haunting me. Could it be that the answer truly was a simple, obvious one? Did we indeed have Portuguese roots? If we didn't, why in the world would our peo-ple have come up with such a strange heritage? Why not En-glish? Or Irish? Or even Spanish? Why Portuguese, arguably the least believable of all? No, there had to be a basis for the claim.

Determined to get as close to the truth as possible, I first set up an imaginary scenario that would give direction to my re-search and reading. I assumed several "conditions" that had to, at least in my opinion, parallel the original circumstances of the first Melungeons, and result in a present-day population of the size and characteristics associated with them. In order of prior-ity, those conditions were as follows.

First, I assumed the Melungeons were telling the truth, that is, that they were indeed Portuguese, and, consequently, prob-ably Spanish as well. Or they at least had a strong connection to the Portuguese, in effect encouraging them to claim such a heritage.

Second, since they reportedly spoke an Elizabethan dialect, I assumed they had either arrived in the mid- to late-1500s, or had somehow learned to speak English from someone who had arrived during that time period.

Third, since their English was broken and not fluent as one would expect for a "mother tongue," I assumed they were not English, but instead had picked up the language and the sur-names for survival's sake.

Fourth, given a known Melungeon population in the late 1700s of a minimum of 1,000 people, possibly as high as 2,000, coupled with a possible arrival date during the Elizabethan period, an average of four surviving childen per couple, and the death of older members, I "backtracked" to an original popula-tion in the range of minimally 200 people, including both men and women. Admittedly much of this was guesswork, and certainly I had no formal training in population studies, but at this point I was entirely on my own.

Fifth, given the surviving Mediterranean characteristics, I further hypothesized that both genders of the original settling group must have possessed Melungeon genes, whatever their ethnic nature. Otherwise, over a four-hundred-year period the Melungeon's dominating Mediterranean physical characteristics would have most likely been "bred out" through successive inter-marriage with Native Americans. Whoever these people were, at least some of them had likely come as intact Melungeon families.

The sixth had to do with the meaning of the term "Melungeon" itself: it had always been a mystery. Even the spelling—"Melungeon"—is a modern-day attempt to phonetically represent the original sound. The Melungeons themselves probably could not write, at least in the 1750s. Most researchers assumed it was a variation of the French *mélange* meaning "mixture," or the Greek μέλας *melas*, meaning "dark" or "black." Others had discovered the Afro-Portuguese word *melungo* or *mulango*, supposedly translated "shipmate" or "comrade," but could draw no direct correlation to "Melungeon." The standing opinion also seemed to be that, since the Melungeon people resented being called "Melungeon," the word could not have originated with them. For my purposes, I assumed the opposite: that it must have originated with them, that a connection must somehow exist with the Afro-Portuguese word *melungo*, and that the Melungeon people only came to resent the word after it was used in a derogatory and legally discriminatory manner against them.

The Journey Begins

Armed with these six premises I set out on the research journey of a lifetime. I read everything I could get my hands on that was even remotely related to pre-seventeenth century explorations of the New World. What I couldn't locate in local libraries and by interlibrary loan, I purchased through special orders. I read anything and everything I felt might shed some light on the mystery. Each new discovery led to yet another unforeseen connection, until I finally arrived at my first theory, a theory so simple and logical that the biggest mystery regarding the Melungeons was that there was ever a mystery in the first place. It is a theory that, in fact, had been offered in unrelated bits and pieces over the years by previous researchers. With confidence in my theory bolstered by the knowledge that others had also come to similar conclusions, I took my evidence to those I felt were more qualified than I was to assess its validity—local university scholars and researchers.

A Rude Awakening

My premise was not received with the interest I had anticipated. In fact, I got absolutely nowhere.

I then entered phase two of my effort, seeking assistance from scholars elsewhere by telephone and mail. With two appreciated exceptions, no one returned my telephone calls or responded to my letters. I even tried faxing my materials to history and anthropology departments, but still got no response. It was emotionally devastating when I recognized I could not even *give* the project away. In retrospect, I suppose the theory was too bizarre and, in reluctant fairness, I probably did seem like a "nut case," someone with whom no respectable academician would want to be associated. Academic reputations are built with great effort and usually by being somewhat conservative. Risk is not a typical attribute of the successful scholar, and great care must be exercised before jumping on just anyone's "theoretical bandwagon." Today I understand this far better than I did then, and I blame myself for not knowing the right "buttons" to push in order to attract competent help. I also had not approached the right scholars, those willing to take "risks of association." Our committee is now loaded with such "risk takers."

At that early point all I wanted to do was to turn the project over to others who could take it, control it, run with it, prove it or disprove it, and enjoy all the academic recognition that would come with it. But I simply had no takers. None at all. Six months later, frustrated and increasingly depressed, I decided to publish the theory myself, hoping a printed version might miraculously capture some scholar's attention, a knight in shining armor who through my ignorance of the field I had overlooked. I typed up my evidence and mailed the resultant article and supporting data to four appropriate scholarly journals, and crossed my fingers. Three rejected the article with short but polite notes and one never responded. One note, while civil, included the phrases "overly exotic," and "highly unlikely," which cut deeply. I silently revisited the rationale for doing this thing, wondering if God was trying to tell me something. So I prayed, and the next morning I had the answer in the guise of a regional magazine that had carried an earlier article on the Melungeons.

Kurt Rheimheimer, editor of the regional travel, history, and culture magazine *Blue Ridge Country*, was kind enough to accept my amateurish attempt at historical research. "The Melungeon Mystery Solved" (Kurt renamed the article from my less confident title "The Melungeons Revisited") was published in the July/August 1992 issue of *Blue Ridge Country*. Kurt had published an earlier article on the Melungeon mystery, "In Search of the Melungeons," by Joan Schroeder (July/August 1991) and I thought, correctly as it turned out, that he might lend a sympathetic ear to my maniacal ravings. Kurt's early interest and support proved to be the inspirational acorn from which the Melungeon oak grew.

The response to the article was staggering. During a three-month period, more than three hundred people wrote letters requesting more information, and another one hundred and fifty tracked me down by telephone. It was obvious a multitude of people had been silently struggling with the same set of familial circumstances, and that I had indeed hit upon a sympathetic nerve. While I had intended to leave the matter at that single article, the emotional response—people moved to tears over the telephone—made it abundantly clear that I had no choice but to complete what I had started.

The genealogies, photographs, and family legends that interested readers shared were not only a goldmine for my research, but convincing proof that the story absolutely had to be told, and thoroughly researched from a multidisciplinary approach. It was too expansive a project to be managed by a single person with a single set of skills. That single-vision approach had always led previous researchers to the same dead end. I was not interested in keeping my work to myself. The Melungeon story belongs to thousands of people, and it will take the cooperation of thousands to solve it, or at least better understand it. That is when I determined, come hell or high water as we say in the mountains, to create the Melungeon Research Committee.

The Melungeon Research Committee

One institution that, out of inexplicable oversight coupled with borderline stupidity, I had not earlier contacted was the University of Tennessee in Knoxville, an outstanding university (and my alma mater) right in the heart of Melungeon country. Perhaps my emotional proximity to U.T.K. had blinded me, but I remain embarrassed over my tardiness in "going home" for help. Better late than never. My good friend and a Cherokee descendant Vice-Chancellor Jack Williams put me in contact with Dr. Jefferson Chapman, research associate professor and the director of the Frank H. McClung Museum, who provided early encouragement and moral support. I was invited to give a public lecture at the university, and this opportunity led to additional contacts.

Dr. Chapmen also put me in touch with Spanish historian and research writer Eloy Gallegos, who was busy writing a book on the extensive sixteenth-century Spanish settlements in the southeastern United States. Eloy was particularly helpful and was able to add immensely to my understanding of how Portuguese settlers could have arrived on our shores. Indeed, Eloy's already considerable research on the southeastern Spanish settlements provided a good start in compiling the evidence I needed to support my theory of the Melungeons' ethnic makeup. His counsel also aided in expanding my theory of how at least some of the "Melungeon stock" might have made its way to our shores. This early support truly saved the day, and the University of Tennessee, through Jack Williams's office, served as the first official home to the Melungeon Research Committee. Clinch Valley College of the University of Virginia in Wise, Virginia has since assumed this role, given my return to Wise County.

It was obvious that previous attempts at exploring the Melungeon mystery had suffered from a lack of a multidisciplinary approach and, more often than not, had been the fragmented research efforts of no more than one or two interested individuals. And many of these lone researchers seemed reluctant to share their knowledge with others, secreting away their findings like a miser hoarding his gold. My aim was to create a broader, open committee representing many disciplines, with a mission to widely canvass dozens of research areas, compare and contrast the results across the various disciplines, share the findings with one another, and then tie together the varying pieces of information. The multidisciplinary approach was ideal for the Melungeon trek and, excitedly, it immediately began to produce results. Although the work of the Committee continues at the time of the publication of this book, and changes and refinements to our work undoubtedly lie ahead, its work has produced evidence to lead me personally to a theory of origin that I feel is more promising than others. And it is this theory, a theory I am personally convinced will eventually be confirmed, that I wish to share.

A Proposed Theory of Origins

To truly understand the origins of the Melungeons, it is essential that we review a number of key historical occurrences that undoubtedly influenced their ethnic makeup. Only by fully grasping the major political, social, religious, and cultural events of the centuries preceding their arrival on these shores can we gain a reasonably accurate profile of their so-called "ethnicity." To review these events we must go back in history some 1,283 years.

In approximately 711 A.D., Muslim armies left Morocco by boat and crossed the Strait of Gibraltar to the southern coast of Spain. Although they were no more than a few thousand hardy Arab and Berber soldiers, these brilliant warriors, driven by their recently acquired religious fervor, quickly and almost miraculously conquered Toledo and eventually most of the Iberian Peninsula.[12] Carrying out the will of God (Allah) and the prophet Mohammed, the dark-complexioned Arabs—who served as the officers and tactitions—and their equally dark but more ruddy-complexioned, often blue-eyed Berber soldiers (who made up eighty percent of the army's ranks) went about the business of making Spain an Islamic nation. "Islam," incidentally, means simply "submission (to the will of God)," and its adherents join Christians and Jews as members of the "Abrahamic" religions.[13]

The Muslim armies succeeded beyond their wildest imagination, effectively controlling most of the Iberian Peninsula for six hundred years. Even today, their influence on Spain's and Portugal's architecture, food, arts, music, and language is strongly evident. From exquisite architecture, to the efficient mining and smelting of precious metals, to the judicial processes, the Muslims taught their less-sophisticated Christian counterparts a new and more vibrant way of life.[14] Moorish[15] Spain thrived as a jewel in southern Europe, its conquerors bringing with them a level of sophisticated science and culture unknown elsewhere in Europe.

These conquering warlords had two vulnerable points, however, that led ultimately to their fall from power during the time period of approximately 1150 through the late 1500s. First, they graciously tolerated the religion of their conquered foes. Being devout Muslims, they respected the God-given right to freely worship God (or "Yahweh" or "Allah" as the Jews or Arabs respectively referred to Him) in the manner of one's own choice.

---

[12]Richard Fletcher, *Moorish Spain* (New York: Henry Holt and Co., 1992) 1.

[13]See Warren Matthews, *Abraham Was Their Father* (Macon GA: Mercer University Press, 1981).

[14]Ahmad Y. Al-Hassan and Donald R. Hill, *Islamic Technology: An Illustrated History* (Cambridge and New York: Cambridge University Press, 1992).

[15]The Arabs, Berbers, and other Muslims such as the Turks and Syrians were known collectively as "Moors" or "Turks."

This right was extended to all "People of the Books." Christians and Jews were mentioned in the Holy Koran as being among God's people and therefore no attempt was made to interfere with their worship. Jesus Christ was revered as a prophet much like Mohammed, and Muslims also had no difficulty in accepting Christ's Immaculate Conception. But to most Muslims it was blasphemous to equate either Christ or Mohammed with God Himself. They knew Mohammed was but a man, however special, sent to them by God, and it troubled them that their Christian brothers could not accept Jesus Christ in the same vein. It also bothered these Muslims that the Jews could not find their way to accept either Mohammed or Christ as prophets, but at least the Jews, like the Christians, worshipped the one and only true God. So they were tolerant of the Iberians, permitting them to worship Christ, or no god at all for that matter, and this tolerance permitted the Iberians both to maintain a separate sense of identity and slowly but surely to rebuild their national fervor for reconquest of the homeland.

The second Achilles' heel of the conquering Muslims was the discrimination on the part of the Arab officers and national leadership toward their more numerous Berber compatriots. After conquering both Spain and Portugal, the Berbers were of little continued use to their Arab sponsors. The best lands were assigned to Arabs, not Berbers, and most real power rested with the Arab minority. Disgruntled, most Berbers took the least desirable, more mountainous lands in northern Spain and Portugal, and fairly duplicated the lives they had known in the Atlas Mountains of Morocco.

The first serious revolt among the Spanish Berbers occurred in 740 A.D., scarcely twenty years after their initial victories as a conquering army.[16] Over the years, these Iberian mountaineers grew to resent the Arab power that had used them for the purpose of conquering these new lands, but now treated them as second-class citizens, both in Spain and in their North African homeland. Predictably, the Berbers became a thorn in the side

---

[16]Fletcher, *Moorish Spain,* 27.

of Moorish Spain, always rebelling, seldom following orders, and, along with the festering hotbed of Christianity, becoming a serious threat to Arab rule. So the combined flaws of religious toleration and bias against the Berbers led to the eventual collapse of Moorish Spain.

Like the celebrated fall of the Roman Empire, the collapse did not occur overnight. It took centuries and the war was fought on many fronts by such renowned leaders as King Alphonso and his valiant warrior El Cid. Parts of Moorish Spain held out until the late 1500s, but, by about 1200 A.D., most of the Islamic control was removed in the "Reconquest." Nearly all Arab leadership fled the Iberian peninsula, but some Arabs and nearly all Berbers remained behind. After all, with their ancestors these people had by this time been in Spain and Portugal for five hundred years or longer. They considered themselves Spanish or Portuguese, many had Iberian surnames, and the lands of their origin were distant places they knew very little about. Some 500,000 of them, in fact, lived on the peninsula and were referred to by their native Iberian neighbors as "Mudejars" or "settled" Moors.

Following the Reconquest about 1200 A.D., an uneasy truce was observed, during which time the Spanish and Portuguese Moors did their best to blend in with their Hispanic neighbors. In greater numbers they intermarried, converted to Christianity, adopted Spanish and Portuguese names, kept a low profile, and generally spoke Arabic or Berber only in the home. This worked for a while, but on 11 February 1502, under the reign of King Ferdinand of Spain, the first throes of the Moorish arm of the Spanish Inquisition began (a decade before, the Inquisition had targeted the Jews and the Moors of Granada). With the encouragement and blessing of the Catholic Church, forced baptisms of the Moors, or "conversos" as both Muslim and Jewish converts were known, began. The Inquisition quickly escalated until 1568 when simple political and social pressure became brute force. By 1582, under King Phillip II, thousands of Moors, including many conversos, were being exiled, with a significant number garroted and burned at the stake. During this same time period, the Portuguese kings Joao (John) III, Sabastiao (Sabastian), and Phillip

III were engaging in the same anti-Moor activities in Portugal. In fact, Portugal's Inquisition was far more vicious than Spain's. Historian Major Arthur Griffiths stated that the *autos-da-fé* (literally, "acts of faith," but referring to Inquisition judgments and executions) "were frequent, and on a scale hardly known in Spain." The final execution for heresy against the church did not occur until 1826.[17]

Researchers Anna Skybova and Miroslav Hroch report that from 1530 to 1609, 5,000 people (seventy percent "Moriscoes" or Spanish Moors and thirty percent Jews) were tried in Valencia alone.[18] In 1565, Giovanni Soranzo, a Venetian (Italian) Legate, reported back to his court that

> It is true that the Inquistion intervenes in all affairs, regardless of rank or status; it is the true lord ruling and reigning over Spain.[19]

It was a time of great horror and inhumanity, akin to the early American witchhunts, the wholesale slaughter of the Russian kulaks, or the Jewish Holocaust. Streams of escaping or exiled Moors made their way abroad, and historical records even depict a shipload of these hapless people seeking asylum in India, vainly claiming to be "sunburned Portuguese" in an effort to explain their ruddy complexions. However, the Catholic friar at Bombay, upon hearing their plea, knew better and denied them entry.[20]

Large numbers of Christianized Moriscoes were permitted to emigrate to the Canary Islands, and found final refuge there.[21]

---

[17]Arthur Griffiths, *In Spanish Prisons: Persecution and Punishment, 1478–1878* (New York: Dorset Press, 1991) 113.

[18]Anna Skybova and Miroslav Hroch, *Ecclesia Militans: The Inquisition* (New York: Dorset Press, 1990) 126.

[19]Ibid., 107.

[20]Charles R. Boxer, in *The History of Human Society: The Portuguese Seaborn Empire, 1915–1825*, ed. J. H. Plumb (New York: Alfred A. Knopf, 1969) 253.

[21]William D. Phillips, Jr. and Carla Rahn Phillips, *The Worlds of Christopher Columbus* (New York: Cambridge University Press, 1992)

Thousands of others made their way to France, as well as Tunisia and Morocco in North Africa.[22] And through those who went to North Africa, vengeance—at least to some degree—was finally extracted against the Spanish and Portuguese who had exiled them. In North Africa the Berbers who had escaped the Inquisition often joined with the Moorish and Turkish pirates of the Barbary (Berber) Coast to wreak havoc on their former oppressors. These "Barbary Pirates" attacked the coasts of Southern Spain and Portugal with great ferocity.

Moorish and Turkish naval heroes soon evolved, most notably two dark-skinned, red-haired Moorish brothers, Khidr and 'Arūj. Khidr, who later took the name Khayr al-Di (anglicized as Khaireddin) and outlived 'Arūj by almost thirty years, was known to Europeans as Barbarossa, literally "Redbeard." From the very early 1500s until almost 1546 (but 'Arūj died in 1518) the brothers Barbarossa fought the Spanish at every opportunity along the North African coast. The Spanish and Portuguese continued to wage naval warfare against the unrelenting Moors and the Ottoman (Turkish) Empire well into the 1600s, with both sides filling their galleys with oarsmen captured from each other.[23]

Meanwhile, in the New World . . .

Also during this time period, the Spanish and Portuguese were laying claim to the New World. South America, the Caribbean, and Florida were the focus of heavy Spanish and Portuguese colonization, and historians have paid much attention to this vast effort. Less attention, however, has been paid to the substantial settlements by the Spanish in Georgia and the Carolinas. One such settlement, a colony consisting of hundreds, if not thousands of Iberian men, women, and children, was Santa

---

60.

[22]Jan Read, *The Moors in Spain and Portugal* (Totawa NJ: Rowman and Littlefield, 1974) 220-31.

[23]Lord Kinross, *The Ottoman Centuries: The Rise and Fall of the Turkish Empire* (New York: Morrow Quill Paperbacks, 1977) 217-73.

Elena, near present-day Beaufort, South Carolina, or possibly on nearby Parris Island. Although most present-day Southeasterners know little, if anything, about the Santa Elena colony, it provided the sixteenth-century Spanish with a base for their operations in the Carolinas, Georgia, Alabama, and Tennessee.

Joseph Judge, in the March 1988 issue of *National Geographic*,[24] beautifully describes the everyday life of the Santa Elena colonists, from their tradition of worship to their relationships with the various surrounding Native American tribes. Judge's article also touches on the exploits of one Spanish officer, Juan Pardo, who is probably at least one of the keys to the Melungeon scenario. Dr. Chester DePratter of the University of South Carolina's Institute of Archaeology and Anthropology, a Melungeon Research Committee member, along with his highly respected colleague Dr. Stanley South, are key members of the research team excavating Santa Elena.

The "Juan" Pardo Connection

In 1566, Captain Juan Pardo, a Spanish officer most likely of Portuguese origin,[25] recruited some two hundred soldiers, probably from the mountains of northern Spain and Portugal (that is, the Galician Mountains) and brought them to the Santa Elena colony. Pardo assigned these "soldier-settlers" to a series of four, or perhaps five, forts, in northern Georgia, western North Carolina, eastern Tennessee, or a combination thereof, depending on the interpretations of various scholars studying the question. Historian J. G. Hollingsworth, for example, suggests that Pardo left thirty soldiers in a fort located in what is now Surry County, North Carolina, part of the old Indian territory of "Xula" (or Joara, as it was called by the Spanish).[26] More

---

[24]Joseph Judge, "Exploring Our Lost Century," *National Geographic* (March 1988): 330-62.

[25]Researcher Eloy Gallegos and his wife Anne discovered that Pardo signed his name not as the Spanish "Juan" but as the Portuguese "Joao."

[26]J. G. Hollingsworth, *History of Surry County, or Annals of North-*

intriguing is Hollingsworth's contention that the Spanish continued to operate a fort and a mine as late as 1670 near present-day Lincolnton, North Carolina, although these Spanish would of necessity have been either new arrivals or descendants of Pardo's soldier-settlers.[27]

In any event, Pardo left these soldiers with orders to hold the land for King Felipe and His Holiness the Pope, and then Pardo returned to Spain. Two and a half years later, he once again sailed to the Santa Elena colony, this time possibly bringing the wives and children of a number of these soldiers. Santa Elena, after all, was to be a permanent settlement and a permanent settlement required more than single male soldiers.

What is of great interest here is that if these soldiers were indeed recruited from either the Galician Mountains or southern Spain, then there is every likelihood that they and their families were of mixed Berber, Jewish, and Basque heritage. While they were undoubtedly "Conversos" and practicing, believing Catholics (Spain's policy was to send only Catholics to settle new territories), they conceivably could have been less-than-equal citizens in a Spain and Portugal intent on "Reconquest." Even more importantly, they also would have been far easier recruits for resettlement in the New World than the so-called "native" Iberians, or those from more "pure" or wealthier families.

Indeed, in 1568, just one year after their immigration to Santa Elena, the Inquisition against the Moors went into high gear. It is quite possible that these soldiers and their families saw the writing on the wall and took advantage of an opportunity to leave before the going got even tougher. That young Christian men of Moorish origin were being recruited for New World service is well known. As Fernand Braudel puts it,

> In the sixteenth century, Seville and the Andalusian hinterland, still half- Moslem and hardly half-Christian, were engaged in sending their men to settle whole areas of Spanish America. These areas still bear the

---

west North Carolina (private printing, 1935) 5.

[27]Ibid, 12.

mark of their origins. Carlos Pereyra has perfectly described it. Spain sent all her sons down to this southern region opening onto the sea.[28]

Although it may be pure coincidence, the darker-skinned Spanish and Portuguese recruits assigned to Brazil and the Caribbean during this same time period were known as "Pardos," a different classification from either "Negroes" or "mulattos," both categories utilized by the Spanish military. While *pardo* can today be translated as "black" or "dark," could the term have originated with Juan Pardo? Or more likely, could Juan Pardo himself have been of Moorish or Jewish origin, with his name originating from the term? Whatever was the situation, the idea of a connection is an intriguing possibility better left to qualified historians and linguists.

Of even greater significance than the "pardo" question, is the little-known fact that the sixteenth-century South American Portuguese employed large numbers of Muslim/Moorish laborers who called themselves "mulangos." These were often West Africans but also Berbers/Moors captured during battle in the Mediterranean.[29] And, according to officials at the embassy of Portugal, in sixteenth-century Portuguese *mulango* probably was pronounced very similarly, if not identically, to our present-day word "Melungeon." (This will be discussed more fully in the following chapter.) Of course, these Melungeons were a continent away and from the beginning I saw little hope of establishing a relationship between the two.

Early Spanish and Portuguese New World settlers were of a varied ethnic mix not only in the Southeast, but elsewhere. Marc Simmons in his fine book *The Last Conquistador*, a biography of sixteenth-century Spanish officer Don Juan de Onate who settled the American southwest, relates much information rela-

---

[28]Fernand Braudel, *The Mediterranean and the Mediterranean World in the Age of Philip II*, vol. 1 (New York: Harper & Row Publishers, 1972) 84.

[29]T. B. Irving, "King Zumbi and the Malĕ Movement in Brazil," *The American Journal of Islamic Social Sciences* 9/3 (Fall 1992): 399.

tive to the ethnic makeup of Spain's New World settlers.[30] For example, Onate himself was Basque and a number of his soldiers were Portuguese. Simmons also relates that, in times of peace, the Moors and Spanish often intermarried, producing a sizable Iberian population of mixed heritage. Simmons points out another custom among these Iberian settlers: their tendency to name children for the cities or regions in Spain or Portugal from which they had migrated. This habit could be of great relevance in understanding Melungeon given names (for example, Navarrh Collins, Canara Mullins, Eulalia Nash, Elvas Hall). And in *The Jews of Spain,* Jane S. Gerber postulates a Jewish tradition that is highly intriguing when coupled with the Melungeon insistence on being Portuguese:

> Even among themselves, the conversos in Lisbon, Madrid, or Seville referred to each other as "Portuguese," or "Men of the Nation," and the term "Portuguese" became synonymous with "Jew" or "Judaizer" not only in Spain but wherever these Portuguese New Christians went in western Europe.[31]

Regardless of their ethnic mix, these soldier-settlers, and likely later their families, were placed in fortifications throughout the hinterland in advance of a proposed road to link Santa Elena with more distant settlements. And they never returned to Santa Elena proper. There is some evidence from the documents of the Archives of Seville that at least some of these settlers were still holding the forts nearly twenty years later, around the time that Santa Elena as an official Spanish colony finally died. The increasing onslaught of the British and their allied Indians made life very difficult for the Spanish in South Carolina.

---

[30] Marc Simmons, *The Last Conquistador: Juan de Onate and the Settling of the Far Southwest* (Norman: University of Oklahoma Press, 1991).

[31] Jane S. Gerber, *The Jews of Spain: A History of the Sephardic Experience* (New York: The Free Press/Macmillan, 1992).

Finally, in 1587, the remaining settlers burned the village of Santa Elena and sailed south to St. Augustine, Florida, where Spanish domination was still intact. All of the Santa Elena colonists, however, did not make this last journey. There is strong evidence that large numbers of the settlers abandoned the colony and escaped into the hinterland, and we know that those stationed at Pardo's outlying forts were certainly left behind. While some previous researchers have concluded—without evidence—that there were no survivors, this would seem highly unlikely. In my opinion, such a conclusion is simply a convenient, status quo "finding" reached by the literal or at least philosophical descendants of the winning side of the conflict. Of course there were survivors! It seems ludicrous to expect that every single Iberian left behind was wiped out.

Historians have had no problem in accepting early Anglo survivors among the Indians. So why not Spanish or Portuguese? The answer probably lies in the old adage—usually true—that the winning side writes "history." The Spanish were defeated, so complete physical extermination was the politically convenient conclusion, regardless of the overwhelming evidence to the contrary. They certainly survived in the southwestern states, and—not being surrounded by Anglos in that more-open region—were guaranteed the fortuitous maintenance of their names and culture. Conversely, any southeastern survivors were in a geographical chokehold, with "melding," merging, blending in, their only hope of survival—if that is what one could call it. Until recently, no one seemed to care enough to argue the point.

While the Spanish colonists did have their difficulties with certain Indian tribes, the Creeks and the Catawbas were notably friendly toward them. We also know that eligible Spanish and Portuguese men often took Native American brides, creating at least some permanent bonds between themselves and these indigenous people. David J. Weber, in his brilliant historical study of *The Spanish Frontier in North America*, unlike some others in his field, at least leaves open the question regarding Pardo's settlers:

Unlike de Soto, Pardo planted settlements along the way. He built a chain of five small fortifications with a detachment assigned to each one. Pardo returned safely to Santa Elena, but his path of garrisons disappeared, their few defenders either killed by Indians or *absorbed into Indian tribes.*[32]

Weber also touches on yet another possible source of Iberian genetic influence. In the late 1500s, many expeditions of Dominican and Jesuit missionaries crisscrossed the Southeast, ranging from Florida to South Carolina to the tidewater areas of Virginia.[33] Historian Helen Rountree provides a fascinating glimpse into the various interactions between the Spanish Jesuits and the Powhatans, much of it related to the English colonists who came after the Iberians.[34] Some of these missionaries were lost or otherwise unaccounted for. They, too, could have added to the final Melungeon gene pool.

It is unlikely, however, given their obvious Catholic orientation and their undoubtedly high standing among the Spanish, that these missionaries would have been responsible for introducing the term "Melungeon" to the Appalachians (and certainly not as a descriptive term for themselves). Indeed, socially, if not ethnically, they would have represented the very antithesis of the Melungeons, being very Catholic, very Spanish, and very proud to be both. It is far more likely that the term was instead introduced by others of a different ethnic bent, and coincidentally there are excellent candidates for just this sort of introduction.

---

[32]David J. Weber, *The Spanish Frontier in North America* (New Haven CT: Yale University Press, 1992) 71-73; italics mine.

[33]Clifford M. Lewis and Albert Loomis, *The Spanish Jesuit Mission in Virginia, 1570–1572* (Chapel Hill: University of North Carolina Press for the Virginia Historical Society, 1953).

[34]Rountree, *Pocahontas's People*, 15-28.

Other "Melungeons"?

In late 1993, Melungeon Research Committee member Robert Gilmer, an Abingdon, Virginia physician, informed me of a potentially blockbuster hypothesis. As I mentioned earlier, for some time I had known of the existence of Muslim "Melungeons" in sixteenth-century South America, particularly Portuguese Brazil. These people, usually captured in skirmishes with the Portuguese or Spanish in the Mediterranean, had been transported to South America for forced labor purposes. They referred to themselves as "mulango," or, as pronounced in Portuguese, "Muh-lun-zhawn." History records that these South American "Melungeons" almost invariably spoke Portuguese and on more than one occasion were freed on distant, uninviting shores by their Portuguese captors. In these cases they were generally referred to as *emancipados* (that is, freed captives).[35] One can easily understand the Portuguese and Spanish rationale for freeing such unwanted "settlers" on North American shores, as opposed to their own territories: it was one more headache for their English adversaries to deal with. However, connecting these South American "Mulangos," or Melungeons, with their possible North American counterparts seemed a daunting if not impossible task.

That is, it seemed impossible until Bob Gilmer brought to my attention the fact that in 1586 Sir Francis Drake had quite possibly deposited large numbers of South American Muslims on Roanoke Island, just off the coast of present-day North Carolina.

According to David Beers Quinn, editor of *The Roanoke Voyages*, Drake had captured as many as five hundred Moors, Turks, South American Indians of both sexes, Spanish and Portuguese soldiers, and a small number of Negro slaves during his South American expedition. And apparently the Moors and Turks comprised by far the largest proportion of these "prisoners." In actuality, these Moors and Turks, who were practicing Muslims, would have considered themselves rescued from

---

[35]Irving, "King Zumbi and the Malĕ Movement in Brazil," 403, 407.

their Spanish and Portuguese oppressors. And Drake's plans for these people indicate his recognition of their sentiment. He was considering using them in some fashion against his Spanish adversaries in the Carribbean. Extant records show, in fact, that he had decided to plant them in Cuba as a colony to interfere with further Spanish settlements. However, storms kept Drake from reaching Cuba *and his ships instead sailed northward along the American coast.*

He arrived at Roanoke Island, just off the North Carolina shores, where large numbers of English soldiers—Ralph Lane's expedition—implored him to take them home to England. In order to make room on his ships for the English garrison on Roanoke Island, it is believed that Drake may (and I emphasize the word *may*) have deposited most of these captives on the island or the nearby coast. The only record of any of these Muslims reaching England is that there were apparent later negotiations to send home from England some one hundred ex-galley slaves to the "Turkish dominions." The "Turkish dominions" would certainly indicate "Moors" or "Turks" or "Muslims," and the figure of one hundred is substantially less than the total number of original captives. In any event, it is highly unlikely that Drake would have executed these people, and later English ships were unable to locate any of them.[36]

And, as Gilmer pointed out, the genetic makeup of these captives (that is, Iberian, Moorish, Turkish, West African, and South American Indian) fits almost perfectly with the known genetic profile of the American Melungeons. It would also explain the "Melungeon" and "Portyghee" and "Turkish" connections offered by our ancestors, something that a purely Iberian origin does less satisfactorily.

Along these same lines, historian George Malcolm Thomson writes of Drake's numerous excursions into Portuguese Brazil as well as other parts of South America and the Caribbean, and of his collusion with the Portuguese and the "Cimarrons" (a South

---

[36]David Beers Quinn, ed., *The Roanoke Voyages*, vol. 1, series no. 104 (The Hakluyt Society, 1952) 251, 255.

American mixed-race people) against the Spanish.[37] And here is yet another, more political reason for the Melungeons to claim a Portuguese heritage: the Portuguese, unlike the Spanish, were at least occasional allies with the English. Drake himself made use of a Portuguese navigator. It would not take a genius to recognize the wisdom of claiming to be "Portyghee" rather than "Spanish" when encountering Englishmen in the Appalachians.

Thomson reiterates that Drake had planned on settling Havana with these captured Muslim galley slaves and South American Indians, but uncooperative winds caused him instead to set sail for North Carolina. It does seem plausible, if not likely, that these Muslims and Indians were indeed put ashore at Roanoke, and that they probably made good use of the provisions left behind by the vacating English. The provisions undoubtedly included small boats for ferrying to and from the mainland. By virtue of the records, it is a given that the majority were not taken back to England, and, again, it is inconceivable that Drake would have murdered them. Only weeks later, an expedition to Roanoke Island by Sir Walter Raleigh reported finding no one on the island. Given the desperate circumstances of these people, it makes exceedingly good sense that they would have abandoned the island as quickly as feasible. Why would they wait for either the English or, worse still, pursuing Spanish or Portuguese ships to come recapture them? I agree with Robert Gilmer that if the three-hundred-plus unaccounted-for captives were indeed left behind at Roanoke, they would have vacated the island at the earliest opportunity. And, of course, if Drake could have deposited Moors and Turks off our shores, might there not have been other, more obscure incidences of this nature? Emancipados freed by the Portuguese themselves, for example? Undoubtedly there were.

At one point, Drake had as many as *thirty* ships engaged in harassing the Spanish in the New World. In September 1586, Drake had released many European (Spanish? Portuguese?) and

---

[37]George Malcolm Thomson, *Sir Francis Drake* (New York: William Morrow & Co., 1972) 75, 85, 105, 107, 190-93.

Turkish galley slaves in the ports of Santo Domingo and Cartagena. Drake's non-English travelers were truly an international lot:

> Drake . . . had released from the galleys at Santo Domingo and Cartagena hundreds of slaves of many nationalities—French, blacks, a large number of subjects of the Turkish sultan, and members of other European countries . . . many of them may have helped out as seamen when his own men began to die off with fever. . . . He promised them freedom if they sailed with him. . . .[38]

Quinn suggests as well that Drake knew the difference between true "Moors" (that is, North Africans) and "Turks" (that is, inhabitants of Turkey), and, furthermore, that Drake fully *intended* to leave the Turks to "reinforce the Roanoke colony." Quinn concludes that we can be "reasonably certain that these Turks . . . were . . . genuinely derived from the sultan's dominions." Quinn further wonders "how many of them got back safely to their homelands? . . . Did he [Drake] give them the choice— either to disembark and settle in North America, where they could take their chances with the local Indians, or else to go back with him to England and face whatever future that might hold for them?"[39] Quinn seems to answer his own question when he says that "whether any of them got ashore on the outer banks and were deserted there when Drake sailed away we cannot say, but it is not unlikely that a few of them saved their lives in this way, though nothing has been heard of what became of any who may have done so."[40] The evidence strongly suggests that at least some Turks—if not sizable numbers—did indeed remain in North Carolina.

---

[38]David Beers Quinn, *Set Fair for Roanoke: Voyages and Colonies, 1584–1606* (Chapel Hill: University of North Carolina Press, 1985) 132.

[39]David Beers Quinn, "Turks, Moors, Blacks, and Others in Drake's West Indian Voyage," *Terrae Incognitae* 14 (Detroit: Wayne State University Press, 1983) 97-104.

[40]Quinn, *Set Fair for Roanoke*, 343.

Even without Drake, it is an established fact that the six-teenth-century Spanish and Portuguese regularly used captured Algerians (probably North African Berbers) as galley slaves for both their Mediterranean and New World seafaring endeavors.[41] Since 1432, the Portuguese had regularly used captured Berbers as slave labor for the sugar plantations on the island of Madeira.[42] Is it too much to suppose that as the Portuguese developed similar plantations in Brazil, they also imported captured Berber laborers to accomplish the same tasks there? One can only assume that they did.

In this vein, it is important to note that some of these Portuguese Berbers, or at least their descendants, probably did end up as slaves in the New World. An advertisement in a 1745 North Carolina newspaper calls for the return of two runaway slaves, one described as follows:

> . . . a tall yellow Fellow, named Emanuel, about 6 feet high, six or seven and Twenty Years of Age; hath a scar on the outſide of his left thigh, which was cut with an Ax; he had on when he went away, a blue jacket, an Ozenbrig Shirt and Trouſers, and a Worited Cap; he ſpeaks pretty good English, and calls himſelf a Portugueze.[43]

One can only hope that "Emanuel" made his way to freedom, or at least to the mountains where his probable cousins took him in. Emanuel was most likely either a recent arrival with a Portuguese connection, or more likely a Melungeon descendant with perhaps a heavier dose of African genes than permitted by law. Either way, Emanual is evidence that at least some Melungeons or their descendants ended up under the yoke of American slavery—enslaved by a civilization that *followed* them to America.

---

[41]Albert Hourani, *A History of the Arab Peoples* (New York: Warner Books, 1991) 227.

[42]Zvi Dor-Ner, *Columbus and the Age of Discovery* (New York: William Morrow & Co., 1991) 28.

[43]H. G. Jones, *North Carolina Illustrated, 1524–1984* (1983) 86.

The Portuguese Berbers, and possibly Muslims in general, may have been navigating our coasts much earlier than we have previously suspected. Christopher Columbus himself recorded that during his fourth voyage to the New World (31 July 1502), off the Jamaican coast, he had encountered a galley-type ship larger than his own.[44] A giant "canoe" he called it, eight feet across, with a palm-covered "pavilion" in the middle. The description sounds amazingly similar to the Moorish galleys present in the Mediterranean at the same and earlier time periods. Certainly Muslim "emancipados" would have tried to duplicate their Mediterranean lifestyles in the New World.

Even more intriguing are the people and items that Columbus saw on this strange boat, and his own interpretation of its origin. Columbus had thought the ship to be like the Moorish ones he had seen in Grenada. His son Ferdinand recorded that the ship was manned by forty men and women, and carried a cargo of tools, copper implements, and forges for working copper. There were also cotton "mantelets," sleeveless shirts with intricate designs and "showy colors like those of Grenada." And unlike the other Indians encountered, these strange people wore clothing, with the *women covering their faces "like the Muslims of Grenada."*[45] Most historians have assumed that these strange traders were Mayan Indians, but even if they were, the seeming Moorish influence on their customs would appear difficult to brush aside. If the Moors themselves were truly visiting the New World, either purposefully or accidentally, then there would have beem ample opportunity for Moorish "colonization" or simple Moorish "influence" on the lives of the inhabitants.

Columbus's nephew Fernando also accompanied his uncle on the fourth voyage and, upon encountering other Indians in the Caribbean, recorded the following: "They tattoo their arms and bodies by burning in Moorish-style designs."[46] And according to

---

[44]Paola Emilio Taviani, *Columbus, the Great Adventurer: His Life, His Times, and His Voyages* (New York: Orion Books, 1991) 217-19.

[45]Ibid., 217-19.

[46]Samuel Eliot Morison, "14 August: Fernando," *Journals and*

historian John Dyson, in 1504, during his fourth voyage, Columbus himself

> made an extraordinary find on the island of Guadeloupe. In a native hut was an iron pot and the stern post of a European ship, too heavy and distant to be that of the wrecked Santa Maria. All who saw it thought it could only have come from the Canaries, proof that at least one ship had made it across the Atlantic before Columbus.[47]

That others both before and after Columbus could have made it to the New World should not be surprising. Renowned Portuguese explorer Pedro Álvars Cabral discovered Brazil in 1500 *by accident*. Rounding the southern tip of Africa and heading northward on his return to Portugal, Cabral made a miscalculation that took him farther west than he intended. Where the South American and African continents are at their closest, Cabral unexpectedly "bumped" into Brazil.[48] Are we, then, to assume that the seafaring Moors and Berbers could not have also made such navigational "errors," ending up by accident or design in the New World? Historians have generally discounted the notion, but I suspect the same old North European prejudices have influenced such dogmatically rigid thinking.

At the time this is being written, the Drake, Moorish, Turkish, and other European/Near Eastern visitations or connections remain conjecture, but intriguing, tantalizing conjecture supported by historical, cultural, linguistic, and genetic evidence, and greatly deserving more extensive research.

More Sources for Dark Genes

Melungeon Research Committee member Evelyn McKinley Orr, a diligent and perceptive researcher, has brought to my

---

Other Documents on the Life and Voyages of Christopher Columbus (New York: Heritage, 1963) 235.

[47]John Dyson, *Columbus: For Gold, God, and Glory* (New York: Simon & Schuster/Madison Press, 1991) 188.

[48]Dor-Ner, *Columbus and the Age of Discovery*, 300.

attention another possible source for the Melungeons, or at least a supplement to their population. Nineteenth century historian Henry Coppee wrote of the many Moors that escaped the Inquisition by crossing into Southern France and blending in with the French Huguenots:

> [W]hen the Moors were driven out, thousands took refuge in the south of France, who, afterwards abhoring the Roman Catholic persecutions, became Huguenots, and that of these many emigrated at a later day to South Carolina.[49]

The South Carolina connection is extremely interesting but generally ignored. Coppee also addresses the great Moorish influence on Spain's New World excursions, asserting that even Christopher Columbus's sailors included "men with Moorish blood in their veins."[50]

On a more personal note, Columbus was known to have suffered from a strangely debilitating disease that caused, among other symptons,

> extreme pain in his lower extremeties, sometimes accompanied by inflamation of the eyes that rendered it impossible for him to read. These symptoms were ascribed at the time to gout, but modern scholars suspect arthritis or Reiter's syndrome.[51]

Perhaps. But to me the symptoms appear eerily similar to sarcoidosis. Might the Melungeon propensity toward this illness find its roots in those sixteenth-century Mediterraneans who left their progeny and genetic dispositions on these shores? It seems a more likely explanation than those presently offered—or not offered—by the medical journals.

After a presentation in Chicago to the Islamic Society of North America (3 September 1994) I was amazed by the several

---

[49]Henry Coppee, *History of the Conquest of Spain by the Arab-Moors*, vol. 2 (Boston: Little, Brown, & Co., 1881) 445-46.

[50]Ibid., 445.

[51]Phillips and Phillips, *The Worlds of Christopher Columbus*, 238.

dozen Arabs, Turks, and Pakistanis who approached me with tales of their own bouts with sarcoidosis.

As we dig more deeply, we begin to see how the typical American view of history has been neatly, but prejudicially, categorized along simple "white," "black," and "Indian" lines, or, even more narrowly, English versus Spanish (with the eventual total obliteration of the Spanish). The reality was much more complex. Addressing this complexity, Bernard Weisberger, a contributing editor of *American Heritage* magazine, points to the known diversity of early American ethnicity that remarkably is still ignored:

> [I]n 1643 Issac Jogues, a French Jesuit missionary visiting in New Amsterdam, said he heard eighteen languages spoken in that seaport town, which probably included *Mediterranean and North African dialects and the Hebrew of a small settlement of Sephardic Jews.*[52]

Even in 1643, America was a Nation ethnically far more diverse than the one Anglo historians have generally painted for us. In grade school, high school, and college, from the 1950s through the early 1970s, I and millions of other Americans learned absolutely nothing of this diversity. On the contrary, until recently I truly believed our nation's history, inasfar as European settlement was concerned, began in 1607 with Jamestown.

Robert Gilmer brought another fascinating piece of evidence to my attention. In September 1671, Thomas Batts, Thomas Wood, and Robert Fallen, along with other English explorers left Petersburg, Virginia under a commission to seek a quicker route to the so-called "South Sea." According to historian Lewis Preston Summers, assisting them on their journey was "Perachute, a great man of the Appomattox Indians," who served as their guide.[53] The Appomattox, of course, were closely related to the

---

[52]Bernard A. Weisberger, "A Nation of Immigrants," *American Heritage* (February/March 1994): 75-91; italics mine.

[53]Lewis Preston Summers, *History of Southwest Virginia 1746–1786 and Washington County 1777–1870* (Johnson City TN: Overmountain

Powhatan and Turkish/Moorish/Pamunkey tribes, and "Perachute" may well have shared a Moorish/Portuguese heritage
(assuming Drake's captives had indeed made their way inland).

But what is of real interest here is that some four days into
the trip, near the present-day Virginia town of Brookneal,
Thomas Woods sent a tired or injured horse back to Petersburg
by a man simply referred to as a "Portugal." Brookneal lies in
south-central Virginia, between Lynchburg and South Boston,
and in the 1670s was populated by the remnants of the
Powhatan, Pamunkey, and other related "Jamestown" Indian
people. Was this so-called "Portugal" simply a Powhatan or
Pamunkey going by his other heritage? Whatever the case, here
we have, in 1671, a reported "Portugal" in the employ of Virginia
explorers. A firsthand reading of this account can be found in
Summers's earlier classic work *Annals of Southwest Virginia.*

There is so much more for those willing and able to do the
sleuthing. Buried but retrievable evidences of an America far
different than we have assumed. But this is a small book, written by a novice "historian," and future sleuthing must of necessity rest on the shoulders of others.

In the fall of 1653, a party of English explorers under the
leadership of Francis Yardley visited with "the Tuskorawes
emperor" who told them an interesting story. According to the
"emperor," a wealthy Spaniard, his thirty family members, and
seven Negroes had lived with them in North Carolina for seven
years before moving on.[54]

Muriel Early Sheppard relates the same story, but with more
fascinating detail. She repeats F. A. Sondley's contention (author
of *Asheville and Buncombe County*) that the Spanish were
documentably in the Toe River area of western North Carolina
and eastern Tennessee as late as the 1690s:

> In 1913 William R. Dockery of Marble explored a mine
> with timber apparently similar to that in the horse stomp on
> the mountain east of Tomatla . . . they discovered a shaft eight

Press, 1903; repr. 1989) 36-37.
[54]Briceland, *Westward from Virginia* (1987) 80.

feet square cribbed with oak timber at three foot intervals . . .
[and] explored to a depth of sixty-four feet, when water filled
the shaft . . . there is also the story of an old furnace of
unknown origin, now destroyed by the excavation for a cellar,
and a Spanish coin mold found nearby.[55]

Melungeon research team principal humanities scholar Dr.
Chester DePratter has discovered dozens of Portuguese intru-
sions into the Southeast, primarily between the years 1566 and
1575. Working on microfilm copies of the records of Spain's colonial archives of Seville (housed at the Center for Historic
Research at Florida's Flagler College), DePratter found dozens
of cases of Spain's having sent Portuguese settlers to Florida and
the Southeastern coast. While many such excursions consisted
of but a handful of sailors or navigators, others totaled as many
as fifty and even one hundred Portuguese bound for the New
World. And many originated in the Canary Islands and the
Azores.[56]

My Trip to Turkey—Amazing Coincidences

In late April and early May 1995 I had the opportunity to
visit Turkey, thanks to a research grant from the Turkish government. As a result of the trip, Turkish-sponsored Ottoman
archival research is now under way by scholars at Marmara
University in Istanbul as well as the Department of the Navy
(the curator of the Ottoman Naval Records). The turks have significant data showing an astounding number of sixteenth-century Mediterranean Sea clashes between their fleets and the
Portuguese. And, according to Turkish Admiral Taner Uzunay
there is long-standing knowledge that many Turkish and
Moorish seamen ended up as Portuguese galley slaves *bound for
the Canary Islands and the New World*. The Turks also assert
that their seamen were conducting their own visits to the New

---

[55]Muriel Early Sheppard, *Cabins in the Laurel* (Chapel Hill:
University of North Carolina Press, n.d.) 13-14.

[56]Archives of Seville (st. AGi) cards 11 and 12, 26 Jan. 1573, 13
July 1573, 86-5-19 6nd 256, pp. 35-36, and 139-1-12, 6nd, 321, pp. 5-7.

World. To substantiate this claim, they cite the well-known map of the Turkish seaman Piri Reis, dated 1513. The Piri Reis map shows highly detailed features of both North and South America, features unknown at that time to the English, Spanish, and Portuguese. As a result of such varied seafaring activities, the Turks of today assert that many modern Portuguese—especially those of the Canaries and the Azores—are themselves descended from Ottoman or Turkish "conversos." In fact, blood group O tests conducted on aboriginal Canary Islanders indicated that the Canary population is much more closely related to the Berbers of Morocco and North Africa than to the Portuguese population itself.[57]

Aside from my own experience of consistently being taken for a fellow countryman by those Turks I encountered, I noted a plethora of equally intriguing similarities between the Turks and the Melungeons (and Applachian people in general). The Turks are a warm and engaging people, hugging upon meeting and offering the ultimate in hospitality. Everything they own is yours and they mean it. Their food is strikingly similar to what I grew up on, and my sampling of a typical sixteenth-century Ottoman meal at Daruzziyafe Turk Mutfagi, an exquisite Istanbul restaurant, was pure Melungeon déjà vu. Beef, mashed potatoes, grits, carrots, tomatoes, yeast-risen breads, leeks, tomato gravy, rosehip/apple cider, and rice and egg custard desserts—the very meals I had enjoyed on Coeburn Mountain as a child. And as with most Melungeon families, an excess of food and the constant encouragement to overeat.

I was delighted to witness the Turks' use of a vocal clicking sound with a slight toss of the head to indicate "No," for it brought back memories of my great-grandmother Maggie Nash doing the same to indicate her displeasure or a negative response to something. I have found no other people who practice this strange mannerism. And the old Appalachian custom (which has since spread nationwide) of pulling on one's earlobe

---

[57]Ilse Schwidetzky, *Die vorspanische Bevölkerung der Kanarishcen Inseln* (Göttingen: Musteschmidt-Verlag, 1963).

and knocking on wood to ward off bad luck is alive and well as an ancient custom throughout Turkey and the related Central Asian republics. At the Grand Bizarre in Istanbul I saw Ottoman-style kilims and carpets with the same tulip designs we see in old Appalachian quilts, both versions enclosed in the familiar repetitive square patterns. Cherokee designs and motiffs also appeared in examples of Ottoman art, and arabesque inlaid designs incorporated into the wooden lids of backgammon games were highly reminiscent of other Appalachian quilting styles. An expert in textiles and the decorative arts could make a career from such comparative studies.

But I was truly stunned when I watched Anatolian (central-western Turkey) folk dancers perform what can only be described as Appalachian line or square dancing while dulcimer-like instruments provided an accompaniment that conjured up unexpected similarities to bluegrass. Only the lavish Anatolian costumes betrayed the Turkish, as opposed to Appalachian, origin of the dancers.

Speaking of costumes, in Istanbul's Naval Museum, Cherokee Chief Sequoya's regalia can be seen duplicated to the most minute detail on the model of an Ottoman levant, one of Turkey's sixteenth-century warrior seamen. The Turks released by Sir Francis Drake would have been levants and they would have dressed accordingly—just like Sequoya, complete with turban.

Family living conditions are also similar. The clannishness of the Melungeons is mirrored in the dwelling circumstances of the Turkish family—the closer the better. Turkish parents want their children, adult or otherwise, nearby, preferring a tightly knit community. Having dinner and spending the night with Mehmet Topcak, his wife, two sons, and daughter was no different from spending time with my own family. Lots and lots of food, laughter, and loving camaraderie—with people who even *look like* my family. Only the language separates us, but ironically the language itself holds hints of a common origin. My mother and aunts have always used the term "gaumy" to describe a mess or problem: something gone awry is "gaumy" or "gaumed up." The Turks use the same phrase (in Turkish spelled *gam* but pronounced the same) for feeling sad or badly about something. There are other linguistic mysteries, ranging from the Turkish word *neyaygara* (pronounced the same as Niagara—as in the Falls—and meaning, amazingly, "big noise") to *dilhah yer* (pronounced like Delaware and meaning "beautiful land").

Even more stunning are those purely Turkish words apparently reflected in Native American linguistics. "Tennessee," whose linguistic origin remains a mystery, is virtually identical to the Turkish word *tenasüh*, meaning "a place where souls move about." "Kentucky," supposedly an Indian word for "dark and bloody ground," is little different from the Turkish *kan tok*, meaning "saturated with, or full of, blood." "Alabama" bears a striking similarity to *allah bamya*, or "God's cemetery," in Turkish. The Pamunkey Indians, who resided in the heart of Virginia's cotton country, may have derived their name from the Turkish *pamuk-iye*, which means "good cotton." Could "Seminole"— the self-descriptive term for the fez-wearing Creek Indians who fled south to Florida—be related to the Turkish *sami-nal*, literally "Semites who have lost out or departed"? Could the "Chickahominy" Indians somehow be tied to the Turkish *chaka-han-eniye*, loosely translated as "a strongly built, good, but boastful leader"? Perhaps most powerful is the similarity between the Cherokee people's own term for themselves—*ani-yun-wiya*, meaning "the principal people"—and the Turkish term *ana-youn* (*ana-yoğun*), meaning "the primary people."

The Cherokee word *atta-culla-culla*, meaning "spiritual father of all chiefs," is identical in pronunciation to the Turkish *atta-kula-kul*, meaning "spiritual father of the red men." The Seminole chief Oceola shares his name with the Turkish *asi-ula*, meaning "exalted rebel." A *mico* served as the Seminole tribal administrator; a *mico* did the same job on a Turkish galley. A *hadjo* was the Seminole tribe's wisest and strongest warrior; a *hodja* was the Turks' wisest priest or leader. A hint of linguistic connections can be found as early as 1797. John Ehle cites French explorer Louis-Phillippe's account of a flirtatious Cherokee maiden who places her hand on the intimate area of the trousers of the Cherokee guide and says teasingly, "Aha, sick."

What Louis-Phillippe did not know is that in Turkish *aha* means "look at this" and *sik* means "male genitalia."[58]

Can these and scores of other examples too numerous to mention here realistically be written off as mere coincidence? Turkish scholars have long believed a connection exists between themselves and eastern seaboard American Indians, based on both physical appearance and shared words and customs. This was stressed to me by Turkish historians during our late April 1995 meeting at Marmara University in Istanbul. Such "coincidences," never taken seriously by American scholars, could now be explained by sixteenth-century Turkish and Native American intermarriages, with the resultant cultural exchanges well entrenched by the time the English arrived in full force some one hundred fifty years later. So well entrenched, in fact, that later scholars would simply assume that such traits were purely indigenous. As with textiles and designs, a career awaits the enterprising American scholar who determines to take a closer— and less biased—view of these possible linguistic relationships. I do know this: so many of our Appalachian people who claim a Native American ancestry resemble the physical phenotypes I saw in Turkey far more than they do the representative Native American phenotypes as seen in the United States. And several hundred Ottoman sailors could exert a powerful genetic, cultural, and linguistic influence on the sixteenth-century Native American tribes into which they married. In a ten-minute period while at Ephesus in the heart of the Anatolian levant region, I met Turks whose names were pronounced identically to our "Sampson," "Berry," "Ramsey," "Ramey," and "Hall"—all Melungeon or Lumbee names.

The sixteenth-century Turkish/Ottoman Empire included the Balkans (Croatia, Serbia, and Bosnia). Researcher Charles Prazak[59] has noted a large number of apparently Croatian words

---

[58]John Ehle, *Trail of Tears: The Rise and Fall of the Cherokee Nation* (New York: Doubleday/Anchor Books, 1988) 2-3.

[59]Charles Prazak, "Were Croatians in the Carolinas before Columbus?" *Carologue*, a publication of the S.C. Historical Society (Charles-

among the Powhatan and related Indians of Virginia. Following
are a few examples.

NATIVE AMERICAN WORD	CROATIAN WORD	CROATIAN MEANING
Powhatan	Pohotan	cruel leader
Matoaka*	Matorka	big little girl
Appalachia	Apalache	treaty
Hatteras	Haterias	luxurious
Cherokee	Shirikee	multitude
Catawba	Kotobaniti	those who strut about
Potomac	Potomak	descendant
Croatoan**	Croatan	the Croatian people

*Pocahontas's real name.
**The mysterious tribal name carved on a tree, supposedly by the Lost
Colony.

Young men from the Balkans were regularly recruited to
serve in the Ottoman military and there is every reason to believe that recruits from the Balkans would have been among
Drake's Turks. Interesting enough, these Ottomans from the
Balkans called themselves "Croatan," the same word carved on
a tree by the Lost Colonists! Perhaps the Lost Colony left with
the Ottoman Croatians (the more European of the Ottoman
Turks) and, if so, a long-standing American mystery can possibly
be solved.

Finally, author John Rice Irwin conducted a fascinating
interview with ninety-one-year-old Alex Stewart in 1981 as
Stewart recounted his youthful encounter with some particularly
isolated Melungeons:

> I couldn't tell what kind of language they did have; it was so
> funny. . . . They'd point and show us what they wanted. . . .
> Called a watch a 'satz.' . . . Never heard [that word] before or
> since.[60]

The Turkish word for watch is *saat*.

---

ton) 9/2 (Summer 1993): 18-19; also, unpublished Prazak papers.
     [60]John Rice Irwin, *Alex Stewart: Portrait of a Pioneer* (West Chester
PA: Schiffer Pub. Ltd., 1985) 249.

My Turkish host, Mr. Alp Kamoy (whose cousin suffers from sarcoidosis), took me to the Anatolian fishing village of Çeşme, a beautiful town on the western-most coast of the Aegean Sea to meet people from the region that had supplied the most levants (or warrior seamen) in an earlier time. Aside from the sheer beauty of the village I was emotionally moved to see what can only be described as the Appalachians to the east of Çeşme—a totally unexpected backdrop to a Turkish fishing village. If some of our ancestors were Turks, it would no longer be diffucult to understand why they ended up in the Appalachians—they were coming home. Alp smiled with delight as I met the villagers and saw what can only be described as Melungeons: dark-complexioned people with the lightest blue eyes imaginable. As I looked at them and they looked at me, our emotions gave way and we hugged like long-lost brothers. My new siblings took me for a spin in the fishing boat, gave me *cay* (tea), and fed me well. And they understood the term "Melungeon" with no need for translation—eyes sad with empathy, their own long-standing definition ("cursed soul") quickly laying out the circumstances of my people. As we left Çeşme, I peered at the Moorish castle sitting on a hill within the village, wondering if my ancestors had once manned its turrets. Or sat with a loved one, enjoying the picturesque view and talking of their upcoming voyage, not suspecting their eventual fate. The latter thought bothered me greatly, so it was that I left Çeşme with a bittersweet sense of both homecoming and irretrievable loss.

Finally, on a personal medical note, despite the intense greenery and flowering plants that abound in Turkey, for the first time in my life I was allergy free. No sneezing, no watery eyes, no stopped-up nose. Nothing but clean, crisp breathing. Later one of my physician friends smilingly but seriously offered, "Well, Brent, perhaps you were back in the region for which you were genetically programmed." It certainly felt like it.

Chapter 6

Putting It All Together

How do we make sense of all this? Is there a general, understandable theory of who the Melungeons really are? The answer is a resounding Yes!

I contend that the remnants of Joao ("Juan") Pardo's forts, joined by Portuguese refugees from Santa Elena, and possibly a few stray Dominicans and Jesuits, exiled Moorish French Huguenots, and escaped Acadians, along with Drake's and perhaps other freed Turkish, Moorish, and Iberian captives, survived on these shores, combined forces over the ensuing years, moved to the hinterlands, intermarried with various Carolina and Virginia Native Americans, and eventually became the reclusive Melungeons. I as strongly contend that the Turkish/Moorish element was at least in the beginning the predominant one, explaining why the probable Turkish self-descriptive term "Melungeon" came to be associated with the various populations regardless of their location.

The gene frequency data we have supports just such a heritage, and the circumstantial evidence, in the words of Press Officer Louis de Sousa at the Portuguese Embassy in Washington, is "quite credible" and "quite convincing."[1]

---

[1]As quoted by Bruce Henderson, in "Unlocking Melungeon Ancestry," *Charlotte Observer*, Sunday 15 August 1993, A8.

Certainly if Drake's Turks and Moors were primarily men, as we know they were, the tendency for their children to adopt the father's heritage would be (1) strong, given the patrilineal tradition of the Moors, and (2) as a result of this tendency, would better explain the widespread dissemination of the so-called "Melungeon" heritage. Several hundred Turkish and Moorish men could leave quite a genetic and cultural heritage after but one generation, to say nothing of the estimated fourteen generations since their arrival. Additionally, the accompanying claim to be "Portyghee" fits with both the South American Moors and the Pardo/Santa Elena components as well. Portuguese or not, it would have been the smartest "politically correct" heritage for either group to claim given the circumstances of the times.

Moreover, the physical resemblance between various members of my own family and the Berbers and Turks of today is stunning. I was particularly taken with a recent photo essay in *National Geographic*[2] that, excepting the desert attire, could have been a Melungeon family reunion on Stone Mountain or Newman's Ridge. For example, there is a photograph of a Berber male seated astride his camel, his deep reddish-brown face and hands testifying to his "North Africanism." But, for the astute viewer, the sight of his pale-white calves riding downward out of his pants drives home his probable relationship with the Melungeons: not so dark by nature, but very dark with the assistance of the sun. But through various ethnic intermarriages, this most Melungeon of traits came to vary widely among the people who were known for it. Over the years, additional non-Melungeon admixtures included Scotch-Irish, English, German, and African, although the degree of mixture with these later arrivals varied widely among the different Melungeon populations. But wherever they migrated, they continued to carry with them the stories of their "Melungeon," "Portyghee," and "Turkish" origins, just as, centuries later, many Americans still proudly proclaim

---

[2]Carla Hunt, "Berber Brides Fair," *National Geographic* (January 1980): 119-29.

their Irish or German or English roots, despite the countless intermarriages that have transpired since those first immigrations. My own legitimate surname of Kennedy makes me proud to be "Irish," but "Irish" in no way truly describes who I am.

The steadily accumulating evidence is in favor of a mixed Iberian-Moorish-Turkish-Native American heritage for the Melungeons, and we should again review a few of the key "proofs."

First, the earliest-encountered Melungeons, regardless of their geographical dispersion, invariably claimed to be "Portyghee," and again, especially in the Carolinas, "Turkish." Importantly, the Melungeons pronounced their claimed Portuguese ancestry as "Portyghee," the way native Iberians or captured Turks or Moors would have pronounced it.

Second, the Melungeons were speaking Elizabethan English, the very form of English they would have known had they indeed arrived here in the mid-1500s, either on their own or with Drake's help. And given England's heavy trade with Portugal during the Elizabethan period, we would expect many Portuguese to speak at least some English.

Third, the English they spoke was broken, not fluent, indicative of a people speaking a nonnative language, as English would have been to the Spanish and Portuguese of Santa Elena, and to the South American Moors, Turks, West Africans, and Indians as well.

Fourth, Melungeon given names from the earliest-known encounters are strikingly Mediterranean when compared to their Scotch-Irish neighbors: Louisa, Helena, Navarrh, Salena, Salvadore, Mahala, Alonso, Sylvester, Eulalia, Elvas, and Canara were names present among the earliest-known Melungeons. Vardaman (Navarrh) Collins's first name, incidentally, is pronounced identically to the Turkish *var duman*, meaning literally "everything I own has gone up in smoke." Coincidental, perhaps, but certainly appropriate for this old Melungeon pioneer who suffered greatly. "Canara," unknown among other Anglo Appalachian families, is especially intriguing.

The name "Canara" has been in my family at least since the 1700s. It is nearly identical to "Canaira," the surname of a principal Spanish monk assigned to the Southeast during the time of the Santa Elena colony. It is also pronounced virtually the same as "Caneiro," a small Portuguese village not far from Fatima. It could also be a variation on the "Canary Islands," the way station for many Iberian explorers and settlers heading for the New World, as well as a "dumping ground" for Berber exiles. And Canara was a family tradition well before any of our family could have read about the Santa Elena colony or even randomly selected "Canaira" from a map of Portugal (which in and of itself would have been a highly improbable action for my "uneducated" eighteenth-century ancestors).

The name "Eulalia" (*Yūlyū* or "Yo-le-yah")[3] is Arabic for the month of July and also the name of an ancient, well-known church in Spain, as well as two villages (Santa Eulalia) in eastern and western Portugal. "Elvas" is the name of a town in eastern Portugal.

Yes, Elvis Presley had North Carolina roots; his mother's family left western North Carolina in the early 1800s, taking with them their legend of a Cherokee and Jewish heritage. His maternal great-great-great-grandmother was supposedly "a full-blooded Cherokee" from Tennessee named Morning Dove White. However, White is a far more common Lumbee, Melungeon, and Powhatan than Cherokee surname, and Morning Dove is an uncommon Cherokee given name. Also, the man she married, William Mansell, had been something of a renowned Indian fighter, making his choice of a "full-bloodied Cherokee" questionable. Mansell's family was also native South Carolinian since the 1700s, placing them more in Lumbee than Cherokee territory. In any event, William Mansell and Morning Dove White settled in Alabama around 1820, and had several children, including John Mansell, Elvis's great-great-grandfather. John later abandoned his family to run off with a younger woman named Mandy Bennett (another Lumbee surname). In 1870, John's son White Mansell married a woman named Martha Tackett from Tennessee. Martha also possessed a common Melungeon surname and, even more appropriately, claimed to be Jewish. Elaine Dundy's

---

[3]Farouk El-baz, *Say It in Arabic* (New York: Dover, 1968) 139.

excellent biography of Elvis provides fascinating genealogical background and unintentionally paints a rather convincing Melungeon heritage for the "King of Rock and Roll."[4]

Other long-standing, common Melungeon given names bear an uncanny resemblance to Turkish names: Didima (as in Didama Mullins) is a village in turkey; Alanya (as in Alania Collins) is another Turkish site; Mahala (as in Mahala Mullins) is a Turkish word meaning "great or special aunt."

Fifth, we have access to many of the surnames of the Santa Elena colonists, and the resemblance of these names to the most-common and best-known Melungeon surnames is astonishing. In the sampling below, the Melungeon surname is on the left and the possible Santa Elena/Spanish/Portuguese original is on the right.

MELUNGEON	SPANISH/PORTUGUESE
Bell	Bela
Brogan	Braganza
Carrico	Carico/Carrasco
Casteel/Steele	Castillo
Caudill	Caudillo
Chavis	Chavez/Chavis
Colley	Calero/Calle
Collier	Calero
Collins	Colina/Colinza/Colinso
Gallagher	Gallegos/Gallego
Goins	Goinza/Gomez/Gomes*/Magoens
Lopes	Lopez/Lopes**
Martin	Martin
Moore	Moreno/Zamora/Moor
Mullins	Molina
Navarrh, Vardeman, Vardy	Navarro
Osborne	Oserno/Osverno
Perry	Perez/Peres
Reeves	Rivas/Rives
Rivers	Rivero/Rivera

*The Portuguese "Gomes" rhymes with the English "homes."
**The Portuguese "Lopes" is pronounced the same as the Melungeon Lopes, rhyming with the English "hopes."

---

[4]Elaine Dundy, *Elvis and Gladys* (New York: St. Martin's Press, 1985) 12-29.

Zachariah Goins (1836–1913).
Courtesy Jack Goins.

Elizabeth Minor (1836–1898).
Courtesy Jack Goins.

The obvious correspondence may be only coincidence, but cumulatively it is quite interesting.

The Blackwater area of Lee County, Virginia—long a Melungeon settlement—was known as "Dona" before Anglo settlers renamed it. *Dona* is Spanish for "wedding gift," and Portuguese for "honored lady." One can only wonder if this precious tract had originally been a wedding gift from a Melungeon family to their daughter long before the English moved in.

The "Hurricane" section of Wise, Virginia was originally called "Fernanda."

But an Anglicization of Melungeon surnames may not even be necessary according to Dr. James H. Guill, a researcher and writer of Portuguese and Azorean history. Guill asserts in volume 5 of his comprehensive work *Azores Islands: A History* that the Azores provided many of Spain's and Portugal's earliest New World settlers. Furthermore, he shows that the Azoreans were, from the early 1500s, a mixed group of people including natives of Spain, Portugal, the Ottoman (Turkish) Empire, Flanders, France, and even England and Ireland. Settlers from the Azores would have looked (and been) Middle Eastern, have spoken Portuguese and claimed a Portuguese heritage, and yet in many cases carried northern European surnames. Guill's gook is well worth the reading for those who desire a keener understanding of the true ethnic makeup of sixteenth-century Portuguese settlers.[5]

Sixth, the location of the first-known Melungeons in western North Carolina and eastern Tennessee meshes logically, in fact almost perfectly, with the expected location of any survivors of Santa Elena and/or Pardo's outposts. It would also fit remarkably well with a westward sweep of Drake's Turks, a people intent on reaching the safety of the interior.

Seventh, the number of Melungeons apparently present in the late 1700s (estimated at 2,000 in North Carolina, Tennessee, and Virginia alone) would, in order to justify itself, probably need an original population base of at least 200 in the late 1500s. Pardo's surviving soldier-settlers probably equalled, at least originally, that number, and certainly would have with an infusion from Drake's captives and other Iberians thought to have been in the region. A tenfold increase over two centuries, given the rugged lifestyle of the Appalachians during that time period, would not be unreasonable. In fact, it may be a gross underestimate.

Eighth, the varying physical descriptions of the earliest Melungeons, as well as their descendants, is finally explained when one considers an ethnically diverse original population base. The Melungeon characteristics of olive, ruddy, and copper-colored skins, as well as blue and brown eyes, and wavy and straight black, as well as reddish-tinted, hair can now be explained by the inclusion of Berber, Arab, Jewish, Turkish, Basque, Native American, African, and native Iberian genes into the original ethnic pool. These colonists were a far more diverse group than has been previously recognized. As we now know, simply because one considered himself or herself to be Spanish

---

[5]James H. Guill, *Azores Islands: A History* (Tulare CA: Golden Shield International, n.d.). Address: P.O. Box 1860, Tulare CA 93275.

George Washington Goins (1835–1917)
and Susan Minor Goins (1835–1914). Courtesy Jack Goins.

or Portuguese, this did not in any way translate to being truly native Iberian (whatever that would mean, since the native Iberians were themselves a mixture of Phoenician, Sea Peoples, Roman, Celt, and so on). What, after all, is an American?

In any case, this new understanding does assist in clearing up many old mysteries and seeming conflicts in trying to categorize a singular "Melungeon" type.

It may also explain the seemingly disparate origins often hinted at by the older Melungeons (for example, "shipwrecked Portuguese," Indian, Arab, Turks, Jamestown or Lost Colony survivors, and so forth): they were, in fact, a part of all these people. And fittingly, as Louis de Sousa, press officer at the Portuguese Embassy in Washington, explained in an interview with Bruce Henderson in the 15 August 1993 edition of the *Charlotte Observer*, the photos of my ancestors "would look at home on the wall of a working-class household in Beira, the central region of Portugal."[6]

---

[6]"Unlocking Melungeon Ancestry," 8A.

The Beira region of Portugal itself exhibits an ethnic brew of people with mixed Iberian-Moorish-Jewish origins. And while our recognition of such diverse beginnings is welcomed, it does emphasize the danger inherent to such a complicated heritage. The greatest conflicts in Melungeon research have resulted from those well-meaning individuals who have latched onto a single component of our multifaceted origins, and incorrectly pushed that lone "explanation" as the only one. Such narrow interpretations are not only in serious error, but damaging to the credibility of all those seeking to establish our true roots. We are the progeny of many diverse peoples and cultures.

Ninth, the word "Melungeon" itself has now been shown to not be so mysterious after all. This sixteenth-century term had been present in the Appalachians since the Melungeons were first encountered. Later, when being legally declared a "Melungeon" meant losing one's land and self-esteem, the Melungeons did indeed come to resent the term. But this late-date resentment was somehow misinterpreted by a few recent historians as proof that the term originated outside the Melungeon community. It did not. It probably came to the New World with those who used it to describe themselves, and its very existence in the southern Appalachians for at least two and probably more than four centuries, is so revelational that it could be considered a candidate for the "smoking gun" in the search for the identity of the Melungeons.

From the beginning, it seemed, at least to me, that the word "Melungeon" must somehow be connected to the origin of our people, but I saw very little evidence of a systematic approach to its study. I started at the most fundamental level: assume that the Melungeons were Portuguese, as they had always claimed, and ask a Portuguese, as opposed to Spanish, linguist if he or she had ever heard of the word. It seemed to be the simplest block on which to begin building.

I will never forget my stunned reaction when, after spending all of two minutes on the telephone with Helena Geraldes, an officer at the embassy of Portugal in Washington, the centuries-old mystery regarding the word was seemingly solved. According to Geraldes, the term, pronounced exactly as it is today, has been around for centuries, and was primarily a term used by the Portuguese Muslims to describe themselves. Possibly the spellings—*melungo* or *mulango*—had thrown off those unfamiliar with the Portuguese language. In old Portuguese, the final vowel would likely have taken on a "zhawn" sound, as opposed to the Spanish "go." We see some of this even today in the Portuguse spellings of Lisbon (that is, Lisboa) and San Paulo, Brazil (that is, Sao Paulo). Portuguese is not Spanish, a discovery that was, at least for me, somewhat revelational.

Perhaps most stunning of all was the discovery that the Turkish phrase *melun cän*, pronounced exactly as we pronounce "Melungeon," means "damned soul" or "one whose soul or life has been cursed." For a possibly abandoned people, thousands of miles from home and family, no more appropriate term could be found. And this Turkish term may also be a derivative or counterpart to the Afro-Portuguese term *melungo*, both terms used by Muslim people in dire circumstances to describe themselves, and both terms rooted in Arabic (*melun jinn*, meaning "cursed spirit").

Through the assistance of Ambassador Kandemir of the embassy of Turkey in Washington, D.C., we are now pursuing with Turkish scholars linguistic, cultural, and historical data that may relate to sixteenth-century Turkish/Moorish incursions into the New World. And given the possible Turkish connection to the Melungeons, the first line of Abraham Lincoln's favorite poem takes on a new irony:

The turbaned Turk that scorns the world,
And struts about with his whiskers curled. . . .[7]

Perhaps Lincoln knew more than we thought.

In any event, almost five centuries of linguistic evolution have thoroughly muddied the etymological waters regarding the origin and transitional changes of this word. It may be that we will never know with certainty the precise uses of the term. Per-

---

[7]Carl Sandburg, *Abraham Lincoln: The Prairie Years*, vol. 1 (New York: Harcourt, Brace & Worls, 1926) 53.

haps we don't need to. Still, the question invites deeper study, and we may hope for a qualified linguist to attack the problem.

Tenth, recent genetic studies show an *undeniable link between the Melungeon people and the Mediterranean.* A 1990 reanalysis of blood samples taken in 1969 from 177 Melungeon descendants concludes that the "results are consistent with the Melungeon tradition that they are Portuguese."[8] Among those populations showing no significant differences from the Melungeons were population groups in the Galician area of Spain and Portugal, the Canary Islands, Italy, North Africa, Malta, Turkey, and Cyprus. Furthermore, significant genetic relationships also appear to be present between the Melungeons of Tennessee and Virginia and certain Indian populations in South America and Cuba. Amazing "coincidences," but perfectly in line with what the first Melungeons had so persistently claimed.

This same 1990 blood-sample analysis also showed a ten percent similarity to Native Americans—what one would expect from limited intermarriage. Surprisingly, it revealed no significant relationship to sub-Saharan Africans, other than what one woule expect from southern European or North African (Mediterranean) populations. However, I am personally confident that we possess some degree of "black" genetic heritage, and that possibly other Melungeon population groups would show a greater genetic relationship than those in Tennessee and Virginia. I am also absolutely certain that many southeastern "blacks" share our Melungeon heritage and are—in every respect—our cousins and heirs to the Melungeon odyssey.

Melungeon descendants show a heavy propensity toward such Mediterranean diseases as thalassemia, familial Mediterranean fever, and sarcoidosis. We are presently documenting cases of Appalachian Melungeons with both sarcoidosis and thalassemia, and suspect that our findings in this area will greatly im-

---

[8]James L. Guthrie, "Melungeons: Comparisons of Gene Distributions to Those of Worldwide Populations," *Tennessee Anthropologist* 15/1 (Spring 1990).

pact the medical community's understanding of sarcoidosis among us so-called "Caucasians."

Thalassemia, incidentally, is most common in Portugal, Italy, and Greece, and among Americans with Mediterranean heritages. Sarcoidosis is also present among the Portuguese, especially those with a link to the Canary Islands and those in the Alenteĵo (southern) region.

Azorean (Machado-Joseph) disease or MJD has been tentatively confirmed in Melungeon families in both Tennessee and North Carolina.[9] The North Carolina families affected by MJD were a puzzle to Portuguese medical researchers until the recent linkage of the Melungeons to the Portuguese was suggested. MJD is a genetic condition (possibly chromosome 14) that affects the neuromuscular system (a stumbling gait and flailing arms are symptomatic), causes double vision and bulging or "pop" eyes, loss of voice, and other parkinsonian-like symptoms. Fifty percent of the offspring of an affected parent will develop the disease.[10] MJD is believed to follow "the route taken by the Portuguese navigators in their maritime discoveries," according to Dr. Joana Rosario, and is believed to be connected to those Portuguese who settled in the Azores.[11] Though she died before our knowledge of this disease, my grandmother Tessie Colley Kennedy exhibited all of the MJD symptoms (from stumbling to bulging eyes to loss of voice). She was treated for Parkinson's disease. Portuguese researchers at the University of Porto, Portugal, and at Canada's McGill University are presently working with the Melungeon research team on MJD-related issues.

Behçet's syndrome, a rare genetic ailment common in the Middle East and named for the Turkish physician who has most thoroughly explored this disease which often cripples and blinds

---

[9]Paula Coutinho, M.D., "Doenca de Machado-Joseph" (diss., University of Porto, Portugal, 1992) 107-46.

[10]Joseph Friedman, M.D., "Azorean (Machado-Joseph) Disease," *Rhode Island Medical Journal* 71 (1988): 149-52.

[11]Joana Rosario, M.D., "Machado-Joseph Disease: Clinical and Epidemiologic Perspectives," a lecture to the International Joseph Diseases Foundation clinic in Beijing, 7-12 Oct. 1992.

its victims, has been identified in the Melungeon population. One victim is Jimmy "Ivan" Cox, a Melungeon descendant in East Tennessee who has taken an active interest in assisting our committee in its medical and genetic research efforts.

Turks, like Central Asians, often exhibit characteristics not commonly found among Europeans. Although my "genealogy" as recorded says I should not possess Central Asian or even Asian characteristics, like many Melungeons I do. My unaccountable traits include total lactase deficiency (inability to digest cow's milk), Asian shovel teeth, and the Central Asian cranial bump. And like a sizable number of other Melungeons I was born with the near-mythical six fingers on each hand (surgically removed when I was a baby). Six fingers is also a trait of many Turks in the Aegean region where they are known as the *alti parmak*, "six-fingered ones."

Eleventh, the colonists at Santa Elena included metallurgists and others whose primary task was to reconnoiter for precious metals, and to refine and work them once found. The Moors of Spain, Portugal, and North Africa were known for their metalworking, having in fact taught the art to the Iberians in the first place. The Melungeons have long been known for their silver-smelting abilities, as well as metalworking in general. Some of the more notorious, such as "Brandy Jack" Mullins and his uncle, "Counterfeitin' Sol" Mullins, had documented run-ins with the authorities over their illegal practices. In the mid-1800s, Brandy Jack was apprehended by authorities in Wise County, Virginia for counterfeiting "Spanish milled dollars." Understandably, but unfortunately, his wooden molds were destroyed by the Court. The great mystery of how Brandy Jack and his Uncle Sol' had learned their craft may finally be explained.

John Swift, the central figure in the late eighteenth-century mining operations known as "Swift's Silver Mines," was aided by a dark-skinned Appalachian people known as "Mecca Indians." Today these so-called "Mecca Indians" are nowhere to be found, and there is little doubt that Swift's assistants were Melungeons. Swift himself was quite possibly married to a Melungeon woman, which would further implicate the Melungeons as the

"Mecca Indians." And, of course, the early association of the term "Mecca" with our people is extraordinarily intriguing.

Ayers Short of Dickenson County, Virginia, himself of Melungeon descent, sheds some fascinating light on both Brandy Jack Mullins and John Swift in a December 1994 letter to me:

> Now, Richard M. Hager, my great-grandpa, was appointed as a U.S. marshal after his return from the Civil War. He was a captain in the cavalry (CSA) and a very dedicated german in law enforcement as well as a good patriot. He was dispatched to the Caney Ridge area to apprehend some supposed to be counterfeiters, names were Brandy Jack Mullins and Rainwater Ramsey. The story goes that the two men were well aware of the location of the legendary "Swift's Silver Mine" lode of ore and used it to mint silver dollars. One Melungeon report stated that those dollars if minted were of great quality and contained much more silver metal than the federal dollars at that time. Grandpa related to my folks that he was shown two nail kegs of newly minted money and was secretly taken out to the shed beside the barnyard and confessed that they, Brandy Jack and Rainwater, had used the molds as displayed to do this excellent work. Grandpa was a man of honor and after their innocent showing of these shiny coins felt that it would be a betrayal of the confidence placed in him. The honorable S. H. Sutherland, attorney in this county, made the statement that if all citizens were of the calibre of Rainwater and Brandy Jack, you would need no locks on your doors. An example of the integrity of the mountain people back then.

Genealogist Delores Sanders of Houston, Texas brought to my attention yet another example of early Melungeon silver-working. In the year 1810, Baxter County, Arkansas saw the arrival of frontiersman Jacob Mooney, who came to barter and, among other vocations, smelt silver ore into bars for trade with the Indians. Mooney had four dark-skinned men assisting him, whom the old-timers could not categorize as Negro, Indian, or White. They were called, simply, "Lungeons," and Mooney was apparently ostracized for cohorting with these "foreigners." The details of Mooney's activities, as well as Arkansas Indian life in general, are described in a 1972 centennial celebration history book published by Baxter County, Arkansas.[12] And the "Brass Ankles" of Carolina were so named for the metal bracelets and jewelry they wore, long-standing evidence of their own metal-working abilities.

The origin of the dulcimer, an Appalachian stringed musical instrument, has always been cloaked in mystery, though most cursory examinations have assigned its origin to the northern Europeans who supposedly populated the region.

> The Appalachian dulcimer evolved from this family of instruments [fretted zithers] although, like most folk instruments, its precise origin is obscure. Settlers in the Appalachian mountain regions came from England and northern Europe, and the dulcimers they played were probably homespun versions of similar instruments remembered from distant homelands.[13]

Yet those who have dug more deeply into the origin of this fascinating instrument have reached a different conclusion, one that coincides perfectly with the increasingly obvious Mediterranean origins of many of the "northern European" residents of the southern Appalachians. For example, here is what music historian Curt Sachs has to say about the dulcimer:

> The dulcimer is a Persian and Iraqian instrument. . . . The migration of the dulcimer was strange enough. The Arabs carried it through North Africa, where it is still played by Jews, and from North Africa to Spain.[14]

Sachs goes on to say that variations of the instrument are also common in Turkey and among Hungarian gypsies. It is probably safe to say that the Appalachian dulcimer is *not* a purely

---

[12]*The History of Baxter County, Arkansas*, Centennial Edition (Mountain Home AR, 1972) 6, 7.

[13]Irving Sloane, *Making Musical Instruments* (New York: E. P. Dutton, n.d.) 86.

[14]Curt Sachs, *The History of Musical Instruments* (New York: W. W. Norton, 1940) 258.

northern European instrument, although the name "dulcimer" may have been given to the instrument by the English.[15]

New Light On Related Mysteries:
Lost Colonies, Brass Ankles, Turks, and Powhatans

Closing in on the origin of the Melungeons also sheds light on other so-called mystery peoples. In my opinion, the evidence strongly suggests that the first Santa Elena colonists fled westward, away from coastal South Carolina and then north along the Pee Dee River. At various junctures they probably joined forces with surviving remnants of Pardo's forts, surviving Dominican and Jesuit missionaries, and possibly Drake's liberated Turks and Moors, increasing their numbers. And they undoubtedly took spouses from the various Native American tribes that assisted them in surviving. Contrary to popular belief, Native Americans did not slaughter every European with whom they came into contact. They were at times quite hospitable, and we know for a fact that the Melungeons were regular recipients of Cherokee protection and assistance.

J. A. and Katie Clark Driggers.
"Brass Ankles." Courtesy Myra Driggers
Mills and Warren Driggers.

Along the escape route, for various reasons, certain groups remained behind in scattered locations. The South Carolina "Brass Ankles" may be representative of one such group whose ancestors chose to pitch camp closer to the original colony. Two other South Carolina "mixed-race" groups, the "Redbones" and

---

[15]Ibid., 343.

the "Turks," are probably related as well, although the Turks apparently also claim a direct descent from a real, eighteenth-century South Carolina Turkish-American named Joseph Benenhaley.[16] Benenhaley in all likelihood was probably *Hall* or *Ali* since *Benim* in Turkish means "I am." Benenhaley married a woman with the Lumbee surname Oxendine, and it is possible that at least some of the Lumbee "Bennetts" may be descended from this more recently arrived "Turk." Of course, Benenhaley may well have been attracted to a people who exhibited many of his own ethnic characteristics. The Redbones probably picked up their name *after* moving to Louisiana, as the French in Louisiana already possessed a term—"Reddy Bone"—commonly applied to mixed-race people in the West Indies. The term was never used in the Carolinas. In eastern and central Virginia, the Powhatan and Pamunkey Indians, as well as the Catawba Indians in North Carolina, could prove to be admixtures of not only Drake's Turks but possibly the Spanish and Portuguese refugees from Santa Elena, or both. I have at least nine possible "Melungeon" ancestors with central Virginia Powhatan-Pamunkey connections (surnames of Adams, Adkins, Bowling, Cook, Davis, Garland, Greene, Weaver, White, and Osborne) who intermarried in the early 1700s with other "Melungeon" ancestors who had come north from the Carolinas.

---

[16]Anne King Gregorie, *History of Sumter County, South Carolina* (Library Board of Sumter County SC, 1954).

*"Brass Ankles."   Myra Driggers Mills
with daughters Louise (l) and Grace Lynn (r). 1993.*

Aside from Benenhaley, the Lumbees of Robeson County, North Carolina are a more complex matter. While the Lumbees are undeniably Native American, they probably represent, at least in part, the descendants of those Santa Elena survivors who followed the Pee Dee River up into North Carolina, then went a short distance up the Lumber River. There they intermarried with local Native Americans and also, according to legend, linked up with survivors of the Lost Colony, infusing such names as "White" and "Dare" into their mix. But then, as Robert Gilmer suggests, perhaps the legendary but contentious "Lost Colony of Roanoke" origin of the Lumbees can be better traced to Drake's sixteenth-century "Portuguese/Moorish/Turkish/South American Indian group which intermarried with the Powhatan, Pamunkey, Catawba, Creek, and Cherokee Indians (who, in turn, intermarried with Jamestown and other English colonists). It is an amazing thought and a wickedly complicated series of historical events, but an absolutely logical possibility, if not a probability.

Frankly, such an origin would at long last exonerate the unfairly berated Lumbees who have consistently claimed both an eastern-shore-Indian and Roanoke-Island heritage. My strong opinion is that the Lumbees have been telling the truth all along. Unfortunately, given the sparse knowledge of our nation's

Pamunkey Indians, Virginia. Courtesy Smithsonian Institution.

true ethnic diversity, most historians—assuming *only* an English Roanoke Island connection—have dismissed the Lumbee claims of a Roanoke Island origin as simple fantasy. How utterly painful it has been for these gentle people who, like their Melungeon cousins, have had their personal sense of identity arbitrarily ripped from them and lofted up for, first, racist, and then later, scholastic, ridicule. And their claims of descent from the English "Lost Colony" may also be true. Why not, especially given the probable "Croatan" element among Drake's Turks? One ethnic heritage does not necessarily exclude the other and, as we have surely seen by now, it is entirely possible to possess what may at first seem to be conflicting heritages.

Pamunkey Indians, Virginia. (Simeon Collins family.)
Courtesy Smithsonian Institution.

Charles L. Prazak, a retired Illinois schoolteacher, claims to recognize dozens of Croatian-related words among the Hatteras and Powhatan tribes, ranging from "Powhatan" (from the Croatian *pohotan*, meaning "aggressive, cruel leader"), "Hatteras" (from *potomak*, meaning "descendant"), "Croatan" (from *croatian* itself), and dozens of others.[17] Given the obvious Turkish connection to the Croats (the Bosnian Muslims, after all, are an isolated remnant of the original Turkish conquerors), Prazak may actually have recognized a significant Native American linguistic link to the Turks (though his article suggests a possible mid-fifteenth-century visit by Croats to North Carolina). The linguistic linkages between the Turkish-influenced Croatian language and the Algonquian languages is stunning. And historians have long grappled, to no avail, with the true identity of the "Croatan" Indians, to say nothing of the long-standing tradition

[17]Charles L. Prazak, "Were Croatians in the Carolinas before Columbus?" *Carologue*, a publication of the S.C. Historical Society (Summer 1993): 18-19.

of Southeastern Indians to wear turbans and fezzes and Turkish/Berber-style clothing. Can this truly be simple coincidence?

Regarding Lost Colony survivors, one thing I have learned is that a surprising number of scholars tend to scoff prematurely at anything that challenges previously held concepts or beliefs, and that many likewise tend to rely on secondary, as opposed to primary, research. This has been extremely damaging in understanding the true history and nature of the Spanish and Ottoman presence in the Southeast, as but one example. Historians who could not read or write sixteenth-century Spanish and Portuguese instead relied on the sometimes questionable translations of others for their work. Committee member Eloy Gallegos, who reads and writes a half-dozen languages, has uncovered a wealth of information overlooked or misinterpreted precisely because of these practices and circumstances. How could anyone who personally examined the original sixteenth-century, New World Spanish records (in the Archives of Seville), for example, not notice that "Juan" Pardo was actually "Joao" Pardo? That is, Pardo was Portuguese, not Spanish. Examining the original records does make a difference. And it may "change" history, as well.

A recent article in the *Atlanta Journal-Constitution* also drives home how myopic we can be when it comes to recognizing matters of historical significance. A huge, sprawing, pre-Columbian city lay undiscovered for centuries by thousands of people who lived and worked on its ancient site. An excavation team led by Jeffrey K. Wilkerson, director of the Institute of Cultural Ecology of the Tropics in Tampa, Florida, said that the city appeared to be "of unprecedented size and early date." This coastal city of an estimated 50,000 people, dubbed "El Pital," existed minimally from A.D. 300 to 900, and rivaled the culture and sophistication of the contemporary Greeks and Romans. Despite the more than one hundred mounds and other intricate stone structures that betrayed its existence, residents failed to "discover" it, and instead constructed homes and banana and citrus orchards on the site. As writer Mike Toner, put it,

Under the noses of generations of Mexicans, the ruins of a vast pre-Columbian metropolis have stood for centuries near the city of Veracruz. The finding of this forgotten site could rewrite the history of the Americas.[18]

And after decades of vilifying the Spanish for supposedly introducing tuberculosis to the New World, what should a 1,000-year-old Indian mummy in Peru contain? DNA unique to the TB-causing bacteria, according to geneticists working on the project. "It means that tuberculosis was present in this hemisphere before Columbus came," said Dr. Wilmar Salo, a professor at the University of Minnesota, and the primary author of the paper.[19] It is yet another debunking of what historians have consistently pounded into our heads.

Nansemond Indians, Virginia.
Courtesy Smithsonian Institution.

We deceive ourselves when we believe that all that is known is now known, and that once history is "written," it becomes infallible. The Melungeons are proof of such fallacies.

---

[18]Mike Toner, "Ancient City Discovered in Mexico," *Atlanta Journal-Constitution*, Friday 4 February 1994, A6.

[19]Doug Levy, "TB Here Prior to Columbus," *USA Today*, Tuesday 15 March 1994, 1.

More on the Powhatans and Pamunkeys

While the Santa Elena/Joao Pardo theory explains a substantial part of our ancestry, it does not explain all of it. The history of the Powhatan/Pamunkey Indians is equally important in gaining a sense of our total roots. In fact, it is likely that the Melungeons are a blend of the Powhatans, the Lumbees, and the Santa Elena colonists, with a strong Moorish/Turkish element present in all three of these parent groups. There is ample evidence, based on surnames, migratory patterns, and heretofore unavailable family genealogies that a substantial ad-

Pamunkey Indian. Chief William Bradby. Courtesy Smithsonian Institution.

mixture occurred in the mid- to late-1600s between the North Carolina "Melungeons" and the westwardly migrating Powhatans and Pamunkeys. Such a mixing would have been both natural and desirable for population groups fleeing oppression, and particularly so given the probable common Iberian-Moorish-Turkish-Indian ancestry of both groups.

Neither the Powhatans nor the Pamunkeys were reluctant to intermarry with other cultures. We know from historical records that Jamestown Englishmen early on intermarried with these two tribes, the best known being John Rolfe who married the Powhatan princess Pocahontas (whose Indian name was Matoaka). Kirkpatrick Sale indicates that, between 1618 and

1622, the general incidence of intermarriage may have been much higher than historians have heretofore reported, given the amazingly high number of Virginia colonists who, despite meticulous record keeping, remain unaccounted for. Sale comments that "it may be assumed that an embarrassingly high number of good Englishmen decided to become good Indians."[20]

But the British soon turned on the Powhatans and by 1646, of the original 40,000 estimated Powhatan-Pamunkey-Chicka-hominy people, less than 5,000 remained. By the time of the 1669 Colonial Census, a mere 2,000 were left, most of whom survived as "appendages to White settlements."[21] In 1685 the Powhatans were said to be extinct, but their survivors probably had continued to move westward, intermarrying with other dispossessed people, and carrying with them the English surnames claimed through those early Jamestown intermarriages (for example, Adams, Adkins, Carter, Cook, Green, Hall, Sampson, Swett, Williams, and so forth). Researcher Ben McCary seems to agree, adding:

> Very few Indians were in the Piedmont in 1675. Many had succumbed to the White man's diseases, and the remainder had migrated or had been exterminated by hostile Indian nations from the North.[22]

And if these decimated Virginia tribes also possessed Iberian, Turkish/Moorish, and African culture and genes, then the stage is set for a legitimate source of Iberian/Turkish/Moorish-Indian-African-European "Melungeons"—a true ethnic "brew."

Let us not forget Thomas Woods's 1671 "Portugal." Within both the Powhatan and Pamunkey tribes, Melungeon-related surnames such as Adkins, Collins, and Cook abound, and nineteenth-century photographs of the Mediterranean-looking Pamunkeys, in particular, bear a strong resemblance to the Melun-

---

[20]Kirkpatrick Sale, *The Conquest of Paradise: Christopher Columbus and the Columbian Legacy* (New York: Random House, 1990) 271.
[21]Ibid., 294.
[22]McCary, *Indians in Seventeenth-Century Virginia* (Charlottesville: University of Virginia Press, 1957; repr. 1990) preface, 77-85.

geons. Indeed, the Bowlings in my family can demonstrate a supposed direct line to Pocahontas, and so can other Melungeon families. I honestly do not know if our line is valid, but on the chance it is I have included it here.

Pocahontas Line

Powhatan & (?)
(?)   (?)
John Rolfe & Pocahontas
(m. 1614)
Thomas Rolfe & Jane Paythress
(?)   (?)
Jane Rolfe & Col. Robert Bolling
(1646–1709)
John Bolling & Mary Kennon
(1676–1729)   (?)
John Bolling/Bowling II & Elizabeth Blair/Lewis
(1700–1757)   (?–1775)
Benjamin Bowling & Patsy Phelps
(1734–1832)
Solomon Osborne & Hannah Bowling
(1768–?)   (1766–?)
Sherwood Osborne & Louisa (Levicy) Collier
(1788–1838)
Cornelius Osborne & Rhonda Hammond
(?)   (?)
"Preacher" John Hopkins & Hannah Osborne
(?)   (?)
King Solomon Osborne & Elvira "Vie" Swindall
(1878–1952)   (1879–1951)
William Sylvester "Taylor" Hopkins & Rexie Nash
(1899–1986)   (1906–1933)
Nancy Hopkins & Brent Kennedy
(1929–   )   (1928–   )
N. Brent Kennedy
(1950–   )

Even if it is not credible, this Pocahontas Line does emphasize the persistent claim of many Virginia Melungeons to have a strong Powhatan-Pamunkey connection. But regardless of their origination sites, and in spite of numerous offshoots, by the early 1700s, the primary Melungeon community appears to have stabilized along the western North Carolina-Virginia border.

There are other hints, cultural and linguistic, that interaction between Mediterranean/Middle Eastern peoples and Native Americans occurred. Cherokee historians have pondered the strange coincidences between the Cherokee and Catholic interpretations of creation:

> [The Cherokees] viewed earth as a great island floating in a sea of water. Above the earth was the "sky vault" made of solid rock. The earth island, according to this belief, was secured to the sky vault by four cords, each attached to one of the four corners of the earth island. On this island, the Cherokees were the principal people. The similarities between early Christian beliefs and those of the aboriginal Cherokees are interesting.[23]

The Cherokees also designated their "spirit race" as the *Yunwi Tsunsdi.*[24] The word *Yunwi* bears a striking resemblance to the Jewish/Middle Eastern word for God, "Yahweh," although this may be pure coincidence.

Of equal interest are the similarities between the late-seventeenth-century Powhatan view of heaven versus that of the Muslims, which Drake's Turks and Moors undoubtedly were. The Powhatans foresaw a paradise

> Stor'd with the highest perfection of all their Earthly Pleasures; namely, with plenty of all sorts of Game, for Hunting, Fishing, and Fowling; that it is blest with the most charming Women, which enjoy an eternal bloom, and have an universal desire to please.[25]

---

[23]Laurence French and Jim Hornbuckle, *The Cherokee Perspective.* (Boone NC: Appalachian Consortium Press, 1981) 4.

[24]Jeannie Reed, ed., *Stories of the Yunwi Tsunsdi: The Cherokee Little People* (Cullowhee NC: Western Carolina University, 1991).

[25]Robert Beverley, *The History and Present State of Virginia (1705),* ed. Louis B. Wright (Chapel Hill: University of N.C. Press, 1947) 202.

Compare the Muslim version of heaven, as recorded in the Koran:

> when the righteous arrive at the Garden of Bliss, they will
> have continuously flowing streams, perpetually clean water, a
> permanent oasis, rivers of milk that never sour, fountains of
> honey, luscious fruits of all kinds, and, for men, beautiful
> virgins.[26]

The seventeenth-century Christian view of heaven was a far less sensual place, with beautiful women determined to please their men not a part of the plan. In any event, and regardless of the beliefs they held, by the late 1600s, these various dark-skinned, disenfranchised people ended up clustering in the protective mountains of western and central North Carolina, eastern Tennessee, and upper South Carolina. And there they remained, accepted by the surrounding Native Americans with whom they intermarried, until the early 1700s.

Enter the Scotch-Irish

At that juncture in time, as the Scotch-Irish increasingly made their way into North Carolina, large numbers of Melungeons were forced to pull up stakes, moving northward through the New River Valley of Virginia into the isolated area now known as Greenbrier County, West Virginia. A few families stopped off in Grayson County, Virginia, and then in the 1780s and 1790s, under extreme pressure from additional Anglo settlers, remnants of both groups returned to the forelorn mountains of eastern Tennessee and extreme southwestern Virginia. The "Guineas," of course, remained put, no doubt tired of moving and determined to hold on to their West Virginia homes. To later historians it would seem that the Melungeons were only then arriving in what would become the most famous Melungeon

---

[26]Ira G. Zepp, Jr., *A Muslim Primer* (Westminster MA: Wakefield Editions, 1992) 90.

territories of Hancock County, Tennessee, and Lee and Wise Counties, Virginia.

Unfortunately, because of limited historical and genealogical knowledge, some of these historians erroneously concluded that the Melungeons originated at that late date, the theory being that the Melungeons were entirely a late eighteenth-century, east Tennessee phenomenon. A small, isolated population resulting from some limited intermarriages between whites, blacks, and Indians. A "tri-racial isolate," if you will. The truth was entirely different, of course, with the Hancock, Lee, and Wise County Melungeons being merely small branches of an extensive population already spread across a six-state region. The specific group that settled Hancock County, Tennessee, consisting primarily of Collinses, Gibsons, and Mullinses were undoubtedly members of the Powhatan-Pamunkey-Moorish population of central Virginia.

But there was also some intermarriage between these folks and their Melungeon cousins from North and South Carolina prior to their arrival in Hancock County. By the time the eighteenth-century Melungeons arrived in extreme eastern Tennessee and southwestern Virginia, they were probably a blend of four primary parent groups, reflecting a well-integrated Iberian, Turkish, Moorish, Native American, and Northern European heritage.

The genealogical and migratory records bear out this complicated pattern, although in fairness non-Melungeon researchers did not, at least until recently, have access to such information. But even without access to these records, at least one previous researcher dug deeply enough to discover the likely Virginia-North Carolina origins of our people. Edward T. Price took for granted that what the Melungeon people had shared with him was essentially correct, and in 1951 he had already assumed our relationship to the Catawbas, the Lumbees, and the Powhatan-Pamunkeys.[27]

---

[27]Price, "The Melungeons: A Mixed Blood Strain of the Southern Appalachians," 267.

But none of this should be a surprise. Earlier researchers took for granted that our shores were early on populted by Mediterranean and Middle Eastern peoples. In 1928, the Virginia Bureau of Vital Statistics issued a document to be attached to the backs of birth and death certificates which stated:

> The Handbook of American Indians (Bulletin 30), Bureau of American Ethnology, under the heading "Croatan Indians," says: "The theory of descent from the [lost] colony may be regarded as baseless, but the name itself serves as a convenient label for a people who combine in themselves the blood of the wasted native tribes, the early colonists or forest rovers, the runaway slaves or other negroes, and probably also of stray seamen of the Latin races from coasting vessels in the West Indian or Brazilian trade."

Furthermore, there is clear evidence that Turks—yes, Turks!—were being brought to the colonies for labor purposes as early as 1635.[28]

In any event, the largest contingency of "true" Iberian settlers (that is, those officially sent by Spain to settle the New World) probably pushed northward from Santa Elena until, after several decades or more, they at last reached Ashe, Yancey, Surry, and Allegheney Counties, North Carolina. There they remained, mixing with the migrating Powhatan-Moorish-Turkish people, and other Native Americans, from the early 1600s to the early 1700s. Intermarriages between the two related groups, as well as migrations back and forth across the Virginia-North Carolina border, would serve to thoroughly confuse later historians, professional and amateur alike, who found the varied ethnic orgins claimed by these people too far-fetched to swallow. And over the years the southerly Lumbees and Brass Ankles increasingly considered themselves more Indian than European, while the "Melungeons" of Tennessee and Virginia clung more tightly to their Mediterranean roots.

---

[28]Nell Marion Nugent, *Cavaliers and Pioneers: Abstracts of Virginia Land Patents and Grants*, vol. 1, 1623–1666 (Baltimore: Genealogical Publishing Co., Inc., 1983; repr. of 1934 Richmond edition) 24, 54.

Tracking the movements of Melungeon families is not easy, even for us Melungeons. Since we moved from region to region, and intermarried with so many diverse cultures, it becomes unmistakably clear that while we are still in many ways different from other Southerners, neither are we any longer exactly like the first Melungeons. Time and population movements change who we are. Ethnicity is a dynamic, ever-changing concept—to "define" and pin it down with any certainty may be asking the impossible. It is quite slippery, changing in nature and form with each succeeding generation. And in all honesty, the history of the Melungeons is a strong argument for not attempting to define it at all.

We truly are, at least today, a *mélange* of many peoples, and that is our great strength. We are living proof that people of all colors and races can live together in peace and harmony, and that the resultant blend can be far superior to the individual parts. And we are further proof that *all* human beings harbor a racial diversity, known or unknown, that truly ties them to all other human beings. It is an indisputable point. We are all the same.

Coming Full Circle

So, like a lost and wandering biblical tribe condemned to perpetual homelessness, these dark-skinned pioneers, most likely—and ironically—of at least partial Jewish origin themselves, finally gave in or gave up. They surrendered their dreams of decent land and peaceful coexistence, yielded in their vain effort to preserve their heritage, and simply took what few securities a life of abject poverty would begrudge them. As a people they fell asleep, drifting off to a netherworld of forgetfulness, losing their most precious cultural, historical, and spiritual memories to an enforced collective amnesia. And while they slept, the world moved on without them, wondering why they slept, fully forgetting that it had been the world itself that had sentenced them to such a troubled slumber.

The Lumbees were among the first to reawaken, moving with great force, and against great odds, in reasserting their heritage.

Books on their history, a research institute, and an office of tribal enrollment are but a few of the tangible manifestations of their regained pride. We Melungeons are only now taking those first baby steps toward once again becoming a real people, a proud people. It has not been easy, and it will not get any easier. But those of us who care must take chances and step into the fighter's ring, ready or not. Each new effort invariably will be more successful. And with our growing pride in who we are, perhaps our resurrection as a people is finally at hand. I view all that is written here in precisely this light. To borrow heavily from Winston Churchill, this book is not the end of our battle, nor is it the beginning, but it may be the end of the beginning.

The true beginning was more than four centuries ago. In a world vastly different from ours. We today can only imagine, and remotely at that, what life must have been like for those early Americans. It was unrelentingly harsh without doubt, difficult at best. We also can only mentally contemplate how they must have looked and what personalities they had. Were they all that different from other people? Were they noble Spanish Conquistadors, exiled or converted Moors and Jews, abandoned Turks, Native Americans, or the despicable, filthy subhumans described by Will Allen Dromgoole? While we will never know with certainty the wide range of whatever the truth may have been, we do have hints at the reality. One need only look at the faces of their descendants to see, at least partially, who they were and who they are.

Who they are today, I believe, tells us much about who they were four centuries ago. First and foremost they are human beings, working men and women with families, striving for the happiness and success eagerly sought by all people. Living, loving, caring, and dying as they make their way from birth to death.

Physically, they remain as they were from the beginning: a diverse group reflecting a mixed ethnic, cultural, and religious heritage. Depending upon the individual, one will see the Jew or the Arab, the Berber or the Spaniard, the African or the Turk, the Moor or the Powhatan or Cherokee Indian, the Scotsman or the German, or occasionally bits and pieces of all these people beautifully blended into one human being. A mosaic of human-ity. Look at the photos in this book, and perhaps those of your own family, and then decide for yourself.

For me, our family reunions are now a glimpse backward in time, a panoramic view of how those earliest settlers at Santa Elena or Drake's abandoned prisoners or the fringe-dwelling Powhatans might have appeared. When I look at my mother, I see a Berber woman. When I look at my good friend Scott Col-lins or my brother Richard, I see Iberian soldiers of Moorish or Turkish descent guarding Santa Elena's wilderness perimeter. In Grandma Louisa's face and eyes I see a beautiful Sephardic girl, turning heads as she carries water somewhere in the Galician Mountains. When I look at "Uncle Will" Collins, I see a handsome Bedouin warrior ready to defend his family and its honor. When I watch my own summer skin turn with lightning speed too reddish-brown for a blue-eyed Scotsman, and struggle to tame the steel-like waves in my graying black hair, I smile at the living traces of unknown Mediterranean, African, and Native American ancestors whose ancient, precious lives still express themselves in my countenance. And I know that we are bits and pieces of many peoples and all races, and that we arrived not only when the first Europeans or Moors set foot on our coast, but also when the earliest Native Americans crossed the Bering Strait.

And in my mind's eye, I can see those ancestors smiling back, wondering why it took the children of their children's chil-dren so long to rediscover the truth. But, I also hope they can ac-knowledge that after all these years their descendants have done just that—rediscovered the truth.

Proud to be Melungeon

Whatever the future may hold, regardless of what "truths" may yet be discovered, or what errors in my own work or judgement may later be revealed, I proudly affirm here, and hope that all those with a single drop of Melungeon blood will equally admit, that I am indeed a Melungeon. A *mélange*, if you will. A mixture of many peoples, and a stronger human being because of it. A child of God, and a brother to all men and women regardless of their creed or color.

Having said this, and in recognition of four centuries of mixed anguish and triumph, I happily close the book on the sadness of the past, and open the book on the joy of the present. This is a new day and with any new day can come a new awakening. We owe this to those who have gone before. For now that we do know them, perhaps our ancestors can, at long last, sleep peacefully. And we who are living can, after having miraculously touched their faces, let them slip back into the ages and find a peace of our own. The past and the present are now one, and no laws or human prejudices can ever again steal from us the linkage between the two. We remember who we are and we will celebrate it forever.

> At that time I will deal
>   with all who oppressed you;
> I will rescue the lame
>   *and gather those who have been scattered.*
> I will give them praise and honor
>   in every land where they were put to shame.
> At that time I will gather you;
>   *at that time I will bring you home.*   —Zeph 3:19-20a NIV

Appendix

Common Melungeon and Related Surnames

To assist those seeking their family roots, I have listed here the most common Melungeon and Melungeon-related surnames encountered in my own research. The possession of one of these surnames does not necessarily indicate a Melungeon or related group bloodline, nor does the absence of any of these family names indicate a lack of such a bloodline. These names are simply the most common surnames encountered and may prove useful to those pursuing genealogical research.

Melungeon-Related Surnames
(North Carolina, Virginia, Tennessee, Kentucky)

Adams	Coffey	Gallagher	Martin	Roberson
Adkins	Cole	Gann	Miner	Robertson
Barker	Coleman	Garland	Minor	Robinson
Barnes	Coles	Gibson	Mizer	Sexton
Beckler	Colley	Gipson	Moore	Shephard
Belcher	Collier	Goins	Morley	Short
Bell	Collins	Goings	Mosely	Sizemore
Bennett	Collinsworth	Gorvens	Mozingo	Stallard
Berry	Colyer	Gowan	Mullins	Stanley
Biggs	Counts	Gowen	Nash	Steel
Bolen	Cox	Graham	Niccans	Swindall
Bolton	Coxe	Gwinn	Noel	Tackett
Bowlin	Crow	Hall	Orr	Taylor
Bowling	Cumba	Hammond	Osborn	Tipton
Bowman	Cumbo	Hendricks	Osborne	Tolliver
Branham	Cumbow	Hendrix	Perry	Turner
Brogan	Curry	Hill	Phelps	Vanover
Bullion	Davis	Hillman	Phipps	Watts
Burton	Denham	Hopkins	Polly	White
Byrd	Dooley	Jackson	Powers	Whited
Campbell	Dorton	Keith	Pruitt	Williams
Carrico	Dula	Kennedy	Ramey	Willis
Carter	Dye	Kiser	Rasnick	Wilson
Casteel	Ely	Lawson	Reaves	Wright
Caudill	Evans	Lopes	Reeves	Wyatt
Chavis	Fields	Lucas	Rice	
Clark	Freeman	Maggard	Riddle	
Coal	French	Maloney	Rivers	

Brass Ankles (South Carolina)

Boone	Harmon
Braveboy	Jackson
Bunch	Russell
Chavis	Sammons
Criel	Scott
Driggers	Shavis
Goins	Sweat
Goings	Swett
	Williams

Carmel Indians (Ohio)

Gibson
Nichols
Perkins

Cubans (North Carolina)

Coleman
Epps
Martin
Shepherd
Stewart
Tally

Guineas (West Virginia Melungeon)

Adams	Kennedy	Minor
Collins	Male	Newman
Croston	Mayle	Norris
Dalton	Minard	Pritchard
Dorton	Miner	

Lumbee/Croatan Indian
(North and South Carolina)

Allen	Cooper	Jones	Scott
Bennett	Cumba	Lasie	Smith
Berry	Cumbo	Locklear	Stevens
Bridger	Cumbow	Lowry	Taylor
Briger	Dare	Lucas	Vicars
Brooks	Dial	Martin	Viccars
Brown	Graham	Oxendine	Vickers
Butler	Harris	Paine	White
Chapman	Harvie	Patterson	Willis
Chavis	Harvey	Powell	Williamson
Cole	Howe	Revels	Wood
Coleman	Johnson	Sampson	Wright

Pamunkey/Powhatan Indians
(Virginia)

Adams	Cook(e)	Major	Sawyer
Adkins	Custalow	Marsh	Stewart
Allmond	Dennis	Miles	Swett
Bass	Green(e)	Mursh	Tupponce
Beverly	Harmon	Nelson	Weaver
Bradby	Hawkes	Osborn	White
Carter	Hogge	Page	Wilkins
Collins	Holmes	Richardson	Williams
Cotman	Langston	Sampson	Wise
			Wynn

Redbones
(Louisiana via the Carolinas)

Ashworth	Gibbs	Nelson
Bedgood	Gibson	Orr
Bennett	Goins	Perkins
Butters	Green	Pinder
Buxton	Hall	Rivers
Chavis	Hyatt	Short
Clark	James	Smiling
Cloud	Johnson	Strother
Cole	Keith	Sweat
Collins	Maddox	Thompson
Davis	Mayo	Ware
Dial	Mullins	White
Doyle	Moore	Willis
Dyess	Nash	Wisby
Garland		

Index

(States are cited with their USPS abbreviations: two-letter caps, that is, GA, NC, TN, VA, WV.)

Research Is Ongoing

You are invited to participate in ongoing research regarding all aspects of Melungeon history. For more information on a planned newsletter, or to add your own research and information to the efforts of others, please contact the author in care of Mercer University Press. You may also contact the Wise County Historical Society (Room 250, P.O. Box 368, Wise, Virginia 24293) for information on the Melungeon Registry, and the Gowen Foundation (5708 Gary Avenue, Lubbock, Texas 79413) for general information on the Melungeons.

It is an old saw, but nevertheless true: together we can accomplish what we could never do alone.